WATERSIDE
In Derbys.

Charles Wildgoose

COUNTRYSIDE BOOKS

NEWBURY, BERKSHIRE

COUNTRYSIDE BOOKS
3 Catherine Road
Newbury, Berkshire

ISBN 1 85306 566 8

Designed by Graham Whiteman
Cover illustration by Colin Doggett
Maps and photographs by the author

Produced through MRM Associates Ltd., Reading
Typeset by Techniset Typesetters, Newton-le-Willows
Printed by Woolnough Bookbinding Ltd., Irthlingborough

Contents

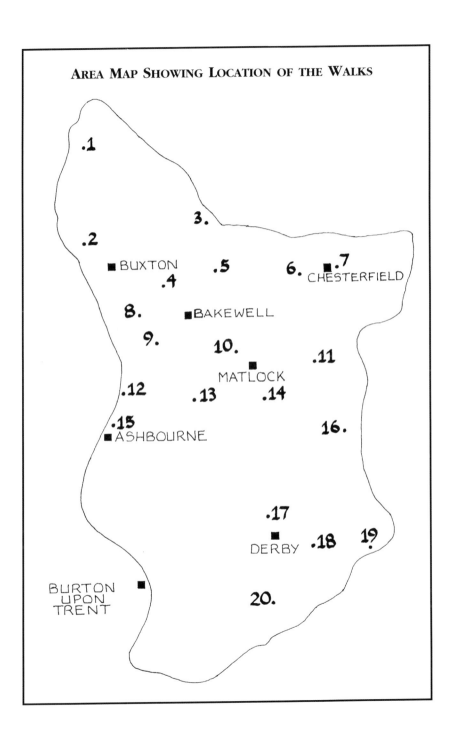

AREA MAP SHOWING LOCATION OF THE WALKS

Walk

*In memory of Greg Boam, Paul Stanley, Rosemary Gregory,
George Henry Flowers and especially Sarah Maureen Peach.*

PUBLISHER'S NOTE

We hope that you obtain considerable enjoyment from this book; great care has been taken in its preparation. Although at the time of publication all routes followed public rights of way or permitted paths, diversion orders can be made and permissions withdrawn.

We cannot of course be held responsible for such diversion orders and any inaccuracies in the text which result from these or any other changes to the routes nor any damage which might result from walkers trespassing on private property. We are anxious though that all details covering the walks are kept up to date and would therefore welcome information from readers which would be relevant to future editions.

INTRODUCTION

I recently totted up how many miles I'd travelled whilst writing this book – it was over 1,000. I hope you will agree that my journeying – which led to the discovery of some splendid walks beside water – was well worth while.

As is perhaps usual with a book covering the whole of Derbyshire it is likely that the eight walks in the Peak District will appear particularly appealing to most of you. Don't ignore the other twelve walks though as you will be surprised how interesting and attractive they are. Whilst the Peak District routes feature arguably some of the finest dales and rivers in England the other twelve walks will lead you past canals, reservoirs and rivers that merit much more attention from the walking public.

Don't forget to take your binoculars with you when you walk. Many of these rambles feature good birdwatching areas and I was lucky enough to see three kingfishers. I hasten to assure you it wasn't the same one three times! The three I saw were at Chesterfield Canal (Walk 7), Allestree Park (Walk 17) and the Foremark Reservoir (Walk 20). I assume that the birdlife is sometimes more interesting on the walks outside the Peak District because there are fewer people around most of the time.

The walks, which are all circular, start near to a pub (or tea room) although in most cases I've given details of where to start the walk other than the pub car park. Please try and remember not to enter the pub or tea room in mucky boots. It only needs one or two people to upset the landlord or proprietor to spoil it for the rest of us. Where it's okay to park in the pub car park it's usually best to let someone know first – ring before you set off if possible. If you decide to opt for roadside parking, do position your car with due consideration for local people and farming activities and be careful not to block any exits or entrances.

As regards pace, I usually calculate that I walk two miles every hour if I'm taking my time and enjoying the view as I go. I suggest you do something similar although after a walk or two you may have a better idea whether you're going to be faster, or slower, than this. I tend to take my time nowadays and enjoy the walk. When I was younger I once walked 56 miles non-stop (in 23$^1/_2$ hours) and enjoyed it (rather masochistically) but now I've got that out of my system I take it steadier. So, bear your pace in mind if you want to enjoy a pub lunch after the walk – err on the cautious side so you're not in a rush to reach the pub only to find the doors are closing just as you get there.

As well as suggesting a refreshment place for each walk and giving brief details, I have also added a few ideas about nearby attractions, to help you plan a full day out if you wish.

My band of helpers is smaller in number this time around but I can report that all routes have been checked and vetted so there should be no reason for you to get lost! Have the appropriate OS map with you just in case though – it's also useful for identifying the main features or views.

Finally I invite you to get in touch with me with your comments on this book or the previous three I have written. Feel free to contact me at my e-mail address *wildgoose@zetnet.co.uk* and I will reply as soon as I can.

Charles Wildgoose

Acknowledgements
I'd like to thank my 'checkers', namely Simon and Lorraine Burnett, Lauren and Eileen Tierney, Pam Roberts, Jamie Wildgoose, Charles Allen (The Badger King), Julia and Chris Gale (still the ML?) and particularly Ian Swindell (who walked seven of the routes) and Balkees (who checked nine of them). I mustn't forget to mention Corkey, Gillian and Liz though. They wanted to help but somehow it never quite worked out – perhaps next time.

WALK 1

PADFIELD AND LONGDENDALE: BESIDE THREE RESERVOIRS

Longdendale is a wide attractive valley between the wilder hills of the Dark Peak, and is the setting for five reservoirs, no less. This very enjoyable walk visits three of the five, along waterside paths with splendid views.

Rhodeswood Reservoir

Padfield is an old millworkers' village about a mile from the boundary with Greater Manchester and just a few hundred yards from the south-western tip of Longdendale. To the north and east of Longdendale are the bracingly bleak moors of the southern Pennines. The walk follows the Pennine Way for 300 yards and also the Trans-Pennine Trail. In fact if you stay on the Trans-Pennine Trail you may end up in Istanbul as this is where the Trail ends once it has crossed Europe.

The Peel Arms is a cosy, friendly pub in the centre of Padfield. The beers on offer include Theakston Best Bitter plus guests such as

8

Pedigree and Black Bull. You can also get Strongbow cider. The pub is open for food between 12 noon and 2 pm midweek (2.30 pm at weekends) and from 7 pm to 9 pm on Monday to Thursday inclusive (until 9.30 pm on Friday and Saturday). There are no meals on Sunday evenings. Drinks are available from noon until 2.30 pm and 7 pm until 11 pm on weekdays, from 12 noon to 4 pm and 7 pm to 11 pm on Saturdays and 12 noon to 4.30 pm and 7 pm to 10.30 pm on Sundays. There's an interesting departure at the Peels Arms as they have a sandwich menu, as well as a specials board. Telephone: 01457 852719.

- **HOW TO GET THERE:** Padfield is 2 miles north of Glossop and just east of Hadfield. Follow the B6105 northwards from Glossop and 1¹/₂ miles later take the sharp left turn for Padfield. The Peels Arms is first left; the pub car park is reached by taking the second left.
- **PARKING:** Customers may use the car park at the Peels Arms while they walk. Alternatively, instead of turning left into the pub car park, bear right downhill to the layby on the right.
- **LENGTH OF THE WALK:** 5¹/₂ miles. Map: OS Outdoor Leisure 1 Dark Peak area (GR 030963).

THE WALK

1. Leave the pub car park and turn right along the road. Turn right again at Wayside Cottage. Pass Peel Farm and continue along the road. Turn left immediately beyond house number 117. Follow this track for 400 yards, descending gradually. Cross the stile on the left and walk away from the track, bearing very slightly right. At the bottom of the field bear right beside the wall. Cross the stile on the left and walk up to the old railway line, turning right along this. This is part of the Trans-Pennine Trail.

2. Follow the Trail for ³/₄ mile, passing under a bridge. About 150 yards after this turn left off the Trail through a bridlegate. Zigzag down to a quiet tarmac lane. Turn right and later pass through a farmyard. Stay on the track beyond the farm with Valehouse Reservoir on the left. With the wall between Valehouse and Rhodeswood Reservoirs on the left keep forward to rise up the gravel track ahead. Pass under the electricity lines. At a path running from left to right bear left downhill, keeping the Trail above you as you proceed. Follow this track for just over ¹/₂ mile. Ignore a

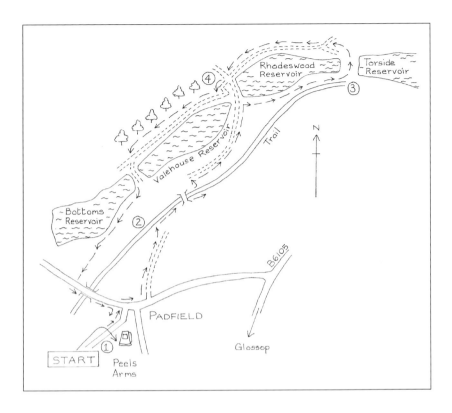

footpath under the Trail through a tunnel on the right.

3. At the wall between Rhodeswood and Torside Reservoirs turn left across this. Once more there are impressive views all around. This route across the wall is part of the Pennine Way. Pass the unusually shaped overflow from Torside Reservoir on the far side of the dam wall. Ascend the steps on the right to cross what appears to be a disused canal. Turn left immediately beyond this along a gravel track. Cross the access road and keep straight forward to follow the concessionary route descending beyond the farmgate. Stay on this roughish track through the bracken. Continue along the obvious route until you reach the end of Rhodeswood Reservoir. Pass through a gate and turn left and then right through the impressive gateposts. This is a concessionary route to Bottoms Reservoir. To cut short the zigzag feel free to use the steps!

Valehouse Reservoir

4. At the bottom of the steps turn right over the bridge and continue towards the house. Keep to the right of this and stay beside Valehouse Reservoir for approximately ³/₄ mile. At the end of the reservoir turn left across the wall between Valehouse and Bottoms Reservoirs. Turn right at the far side along the path. Keep on this for nearly ¹/₂ mile, ignoring a path to the left after 300 yards. The path you are on rises slightly above the reservoir. Near the top of the rise turn left over a stile and walk up the right side of a field. Climb the stile at the top of the field and walk forward to the road. Turn left up the road into Padfield. Take the first right along the road then turn almost immediately left into the pub car park.

PLACES OF INTEREST NEARBY
Visit *Glossop Heritage Centre* in Henry Street, Glossop, and learn about the history of Glossop which dates back over 1,000 years. Telephone: 01457 869176.

WHALEY BRIDGE, THE PEAK FOREST CANAL AND TODDBROOK RESERVOIR

This walk takes you along the Peak Forest Canal away from the hustle and bustle of daily life. Surprisingly it's only a good stone's throw away from busy main roads. It then leads you into the countryside, across the dam wall of the Toddbrook Reservoir and nudges the River Goyt before returning to the start.

Narrowboats at Whaley Bridge

Whaley Bridge marked the northern point of the Cromford and High Peak Railway. This was a high level route (with some steep inclines) that ran for over 30 miles from Cromford further south. The railway line linked with the Peak Forest Canal which heads north from Whaley Bridge and a section of which forms an enjoyable part of this walk. Toddbrook Reservoir towards the end of the route was built in the mid-1800s.

The Goyt Inn in Whaley Bridge is a small pub with a canalside atmosphere – the canal is after all fairly near. The pub is open from 12 noon until 11 pm all week except Sundays when it closes at 10.30 pm. Food is available from 12 noon until 2.30 pm every day and from 5 pm until 8 pm on Monday to Thursday evenings. Vaux and Wards Bitters are on sale plus guests such as Moonlight Mouse's Autumn Ale. The traditional food (for example, fish, chips and peas, chilli with rice or chips, chicken or beef curry with rice or chips) is very welcome after a bracing walk. Telephone: 01663 732840.

- **HOW TO GET THERE:** Whaley Bridge is just off the A6 between Buxton and Stockport.
- **PARKING:** Taking the A5004, turn off eastwards opposite the Jodrell Arms then immediately left again into Canal Street. Follow this to the end. Turn right and right again to reach a public car park.
- **LENGTH OF THE WALK:** 5¼ miles. Map: OS Outdoor Leisure 1 Dark Peak area (GR 013816).

THE WALK

1. From the car park entrance walk right to the distinctive stone building with the AD 1832 date. This takes you along the Goyt Way (signed 'GW'). Continue forward over a narrow footbridge to cross the canal overflow. Walk alongside the canal for ⅓ mile. Where the canal forks take the left fork by crossing the footbridge and following the Goyt Way. This runs on the right side of the canal with (later) gardens stretching down to the canal on the far side. Continue beside the canal, passing under various bridges. There is a hum of traffic to your left but the canal is restful.

2. When you reach bridge 31 pass under it and turn immediately right to cross it and the canal. Stay on the road and use the footbridge to cross the railway line into Furness Vale. Then cross the A6 into Yeardsley Lane. Walk up this and fork right into Diglee Road. This leads into open country. Keep on the tarmac lane before forking left uphill where the lane splits. Follow the drive right through the farmyard. Keep on up the track beyond. Behind you the view opens out. This is a fairly steep path bringing you to Whaley Lane.

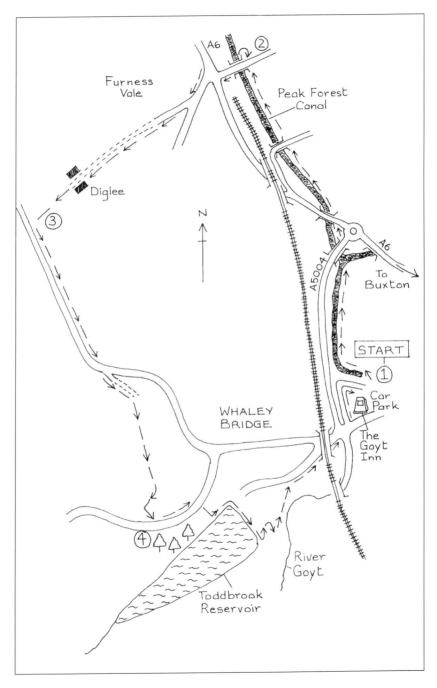

3. Turn left here and continue for ¹/₃ mile. Ignore a footpath on the left and later one on the right (for Bowstonegate and Lyme Park). As the road starts to bend away to the left keep straight ahead at a rough layby along the track in front. Follow this to a low wall on the left. Continue and bear right to the end of the track on the footpath for Hawkhurst Head, ignoring the path for Stoneheads. Climb the stile beside the gate and enter a field. Walk alongside the wall on the left. At the end of this long field cross a stile between the two farmgates. About 100 yards later the path descends beside the wall. Straight ahead across the valley is the ridge of Taxal Moor. Stay beside the wall as it bears right, then left, to a road.

4. Turn left along this for 500 yards. Look out for a bungalow called 'Toddbrook' on the right. Pass this and the next house before turning right down a walled path. Descend to a road with Toddbrook Reservoir beyond. Turn left along the road for 100 yards to the end of the reservoir. Turn right across the dam wall. At the end turn sharp left to descend along a path with the dam above to your left. This path zigzags down into a park with the River Goyt at the bottom. Turn left here. Beyond the playground on the left follow the tarmac path uphill towards the old church. Continue past this to the road. Turn right along this. Pass under the railway bridge and cross the main road in front of the Jodrell Arms. Turn left along Canal Street which runs parallel to (but below) the main road. Follow this back to the start.

PLACES OF INTEREST NEARBY
Following the A6 north from Whaley Bridge towards Stockport, just beyond Disley you will find the National Trust property, *Lyme Park*. The BBC filmed part of *Pride and Prejudice* here with the hall doubling for 'Pemberley'. Telephone: 01663 766492.

GRINDLEFORD AND THE RIVER DERWENT

This is one of the shorter walks in the book but what it lacks in quantity it more than makes up for in quality. Lovely scenery with a stunning view halfway through and a delightful stretch of riverside path make this very enjoyable walking indeed.

Looking towards Eyam Moor from Dakin's Barn

Grindleford is in a lovely wooded setting through which the River Derwent flows on its way down to Chatsworth before continuing south through the county to join the Trent south-east of Derby. On the walk you will pass Padley Chapel. In the 16th century two Roman Catholic priests, Robert Ludlam and Nicholas Garlick, were taken from here to Derby where they were hanged, drawn and quartered near St Mary's Bridge. The chapel in time gone by was allowed to deteriorate but fortunately in more recent years has been returned to its original and proper use – as a chapel. It is sometimes open to the public – check on the door for details.

The Longshaw Bar at the Maynard Arms Hotel is not only close to the start of the walk but also an excellent place to visit at any time. The service is very friendly and something just a bit different is offered, foodwise, such as seared conger eel or apple and apricot stir fry. There's also the more usual fare, spicy chicken curry, grilled gammon and steak and mushroom pie, for example. The beers are good too with Old Speckled Hen, Boddingtons and Pedigree (plus Flowers in summer) on offer. The bar is open from 12 noon to 2 pm and 5.30 pm to 11 pm on Monday to Friday and all day on Saturday and Sunday. Food is available from 12 noon until 2 pm and 6 pm until 9 pm during the week and from 12 noon until 9 pm at weekends. Incidentally, the menu changes every day and accommodation is available. Telephone: 01433 630231.

- **HOW TO GET THERE:** Grindleford is 6 miles north of Bakewell, on the B6521.
- **PARKING:** Park on the access road to Grindleford railway station. This is just uphill (and on the opposite side of the road) from the Maynard Arms on the B6521.
- **LENGTH OF THE WALK:** 4³/₄ miles. Maps: The walk starts and finishes on OS Outdoor Leisure 24 White Peak area with the middle section on sheet 1 Dark Peak area (GR 251786).

THE WALK

1. Walk down the road to the station. Cross the bridge over the railway line with Totley Tunnel to the right. Ignore the left turn to the railway platform immediately after the bridge. Proceed forward through the gateway and bear left on the track. Ignore the stile into Padley Gorge on the right. Cross Burbage Brook and then pass Padley Mill on the right. Stay on this track, ignoring another round the corner from the mill leading uphill to the right. Walk past the semi-detached houses on the left and look out for the railway signal box shortly after, down to the left. Continue to Brunts Barn with Padley Chapel to the right.

2. Walk between these two buildings and enter the National Trust Longshaw Estate, which used to belong to the Dukes of Rutland. Stay on the track, soon passing four or five more houses.

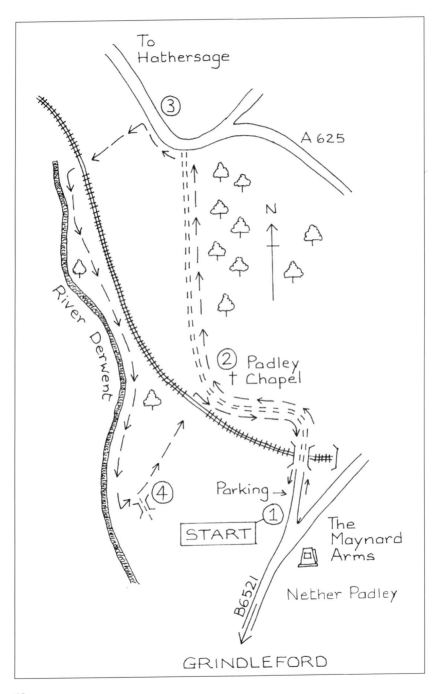

Padley Chapel

Subsequently pass through a farmyard. Look out for unfinished millstones on the right – a good spot for a rest. Then pass through Greenwood Farm with more unfinished millstones hereabouts. Continue up the track, rising steadily until it goes up more steeply just before the road. Down to the left is an impressive view of the Derwent Valley. Hathersage comes into view ahead. Turn left at the road and pass the Millstone Inn.

3. About 100 yards later, immediately past a house on the left, turn sharp left down a narrowish tarmac lane. Pass Fairfields then, at Dakin's Barn, pass through the small gate to the right of the small outbuilding. A lovely view opens out before you. Walk down the right side of the first field, the left side of the second and the right side of the third and fourth. This should bring you to the railway line. Cross this carefully and follow the path as it descends to the River Derwent below. Turn left beside the river. Just before Harper Lees there are some cut stones, remnants of an impressive building by the look of things, scattered by the riverside. Cross the small stone bridge then bear slightly right through the kissing gate. Keep on the left side of this field alongside the fence – not along the riverside. At the end of the fence keep forward through the field in the same direction. This eventually brings you back to the river. A little later enter Coppice Wood – part of the Longshaw Estate. This is delightful. Leave the wood and walk beside the river through the next two fields until in the second one you have to walk left at the end, away from the river, towards a stile.

4. Do not cross the agricultural bridge here though – bear left uphill under the electricity line, do not go over the stream. Walk beside a wall on your left as you rise through a slightly marshy area into a drier, more open field beyond. As you go you will see an old sunken lane beside the wall. Pass through a gap in the top left corner of the field. Bear half right through another gap in the wall on the opposite side of the field. Once through this turn right on the track. Cross the railway line. Turn right along the track, back to the start.

PLACES OF INTEREST NEARBY
Travel north-westwards for two or three miles to visit the plague village of *Eyam*. Whilst you're there you may be able to visit *Eyam Hall* which has been in the Wright family for 320 years. The Hall is a 17th-century manor house complete with stone-flagged floors and is open to the public from Easter to the end of October on certain days of the week. There's also a small craft centre attached to the Hall. For further information call 01433 631976.

ASHFORD IN THE WATER AND THE RIVER WYE

A well known and popular route beside the Wye to reach the beauty spot of Monsal Head. This is archetypal Peak District scenery you can enjoy in every season.

Sheepwash Bridge

Ashford is appropriately named. In autumn 1998, for example, the River Wye flooded, closing the A6 for a few days and causing problems for the local villagers. It's a lovely village, worth walking round at a leisurely pace. Try and see the village church of the Holy Trinity with its unusual maiden's garlands. The walk passes over the oft-photographed Sheepwash Bridge where in medieval times sheep were washed before being sheared. It is still used for this purpose today albeit as a custom on just one day a year. The Tourist Information Centre in Bakewell (01629 813227) can give you details. Well dressings are another ancient Derbyshire custom in which thanks are given for the provision of water. The well dressings comprise a clay-filled frame into which are pressed flower petals and other natural materials to create a 'picture' which is placed at the well for approximately one week until the clay dries. They really are most impressive. The wells in Ashford are 'dressed' every year in the week after Trinity Sunday, eight weeks after Easter. Telephone Bakewell Tourist Information Centre for the exact dates which change annually.

The Mill House Hotel was formerly the Ashford Hotel. The food is still as good as ever. Opening hours are from 11 am to 11 pm on Monday to Saturday and from 12 noon until 10.30 pm on Sunday. Food is served from 12 noon every day until 9.30 pm (9 pm on Sunday). Stones Bitter, Bass, Worthington and John Smith's are all available plus Blackthorn cider. There's a wide ranging menu with Appetisers, Perfect Pasta, Hot from the Grill, Seafarer's Selection, Mill House Favourites, Spice Traders Selection and a Light Bite Selection. Telephone: 01629 812725.

- **HOW TO GET THERE:** Ashford in the Water is 2 miles north-west of Bakewell, on the A6.
- **PARKING:** Park in the small car park in the centre of the village or the car park of the Mill House Hotel – if you are a customer. For the village car park drive towards the church along Church Street from the hotel. Take the first turn right into Court Lane. The car park is just over 200 yards along here on the right.
- **LENGTH OF THE WALK:** 6¼ miles. Map: OS Outdoor Leisure 24 White Peak area (GR 194698).

THE WALK

1. From the car park entrance (with the toilets to your left) turn left on the road past the toilets. Follow this, keeping the church on the right. At the T-junction turn right with the church still on the right. Walk forward, ignoring Fennel Street as it bears right. Keep to the left of the shelter and cross ancient Sheepwash Bridge over the Wye.

2. Turn right on the A6, crossing onto the left side as soon as possible. Fork left onto the lane for Sheldon. About 300 yards later on the sharp left bend bear right off the road to a gate. Follow the path beyond running alongside the river. Pass through a gateway with the corner of a wood on the left. Continue beside the wall on the right to another gateway. Pass through the stile and follow the

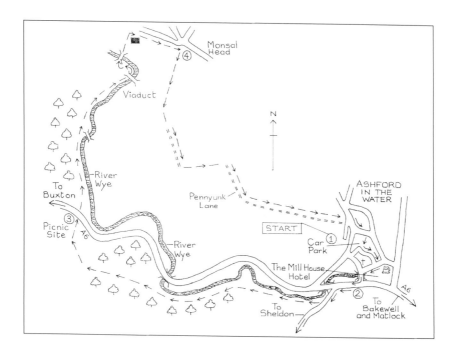

gravel path to the waterwheel. Keep left of this and follow the path behind it. This is a lovely (and cool) stretch of path in summertime. Some 300 yards later water gushes out of man-made Magpie Sough below to the right. This drains water from the workings of Magpie Mine over a mile away on the hillside above. Continue along the path, bearing left at a pond through the woods until you reach a crossroads of paths. Keep straight on but before you do have a glimpse at the 250 steps to the left constructed by local walkers – some literally shed blood on this job! The route through the wood rises steadily until eventually there is quite a drop to the right. After walking some way through the trees cross a stile in a wall and bear half right downhill. This brings you into the open. Where the path forks ignore the route heading forward and slightly uphill. Follow the right fork downhill to a wall. Cross this and turn right. Ignore a path to the left and continue to White Lodge Picnic Site.

3. Cross the car park and descend the steps to the A6. Cross this carefully to the stile opposite. On the path beyond cross some stepping stones to another stile. A few yards later take the path to the right and continue along the main path through the dale for a mile. Keep to the left hand side of the river all the way, ignoring a footbridge on the right as you proceed. Look out for black rabbits – they are often to be seen particularly towards dusk or very early in the morning. Pass the weir on the right until the viaduct looms up ahead. Walk towards and then underneath it. Follow the path beyond to the left beside the river. Cross the footbridge to Upperdale Farm, keeping left of this. Turn right immediately beyond the buildings. Follow this bridleway as it climbs (sometimes quite steeply) to Monsal Head. Ignore a path to the right as you go. When you reach the top of the hill pass through the squeezer stile to admire the view of the dale and viaduct from the car park in front of the Monsal Head Hotel.

4. Return to the squeezer stile. Pass through this, descend the steps and bear left, taking the path signed 'Monsal Dale Weir and Ashford'. A few yards later fork left on the path for Ashford. Follow this for $1/3$ mile, crossing one stile. A view of the dale is visible through the trees on your right. Cross the stile beside a gate and follow the walled path. At the end of this keep forward, picking up another stretch of walled path before reaching a dewpond on the left. Pass this and turn left to walk down the right side of the field ahead. At the bottom turn right onto the walled track. Follow this all the way into Ashford, ignoring a grassy track to the left after 80 yards. This is Pennyunk Lane and is hundreds (if not a few thousands) of years old. Eventually you reach the outskirts of Ashford and an open area of road. Ignore the right turn. Walk forward to the road ahead and turn right along this. Almost immediately bear left down the steep road. Two-thirds of the way down turn right along the path immediately after the garage of Little Cottage. Follow this into the playing field. Keep on the right side and to the left of the cemetery. Pass through the squeezer stile to arrive back at the car park.

PLACES OF INTEREST NEARBY
To the south-east is *Bakewell* with its shops, Bakewell Puddings and the Old House Museum. A couple of miles further is *Haddon Hall* – a marvellous medieval hall largely ignored for centuries and therefore unaltered. Telephone: 01629 812855.

WALK 5
CALVER AND THE RIVER DERWENT

This stroll beside the Derwent leads to a path along a ridge topped by Bramley and Bank Woods. These are enjoyable in all seasons but particularly when the bluebells or rhododendrons are in flower.

The River Derwent from Bubnell Bridge

We've always had this tendency in Derbyshire to spell a place name one way and pronounce it another. Calver is no different – it's pronounced 'Carver'. Calver Mill which you may get a glimpse of very near the beginning of the walk, providing the leaves are not too thick, was used in the filming of *Colditz* on BBC TV some years ago. Plans are now afoot to convert it into flats. The walk also passes through Bubnell with its ancient bridge over the Derwent.

The Bridge Inn in Calver is one of those pubs that's got it right. No airs and graces – just a good pub with good food and beer – what more could you want? They're open from 11.30 am to 3 pm and 5.30 pm to 11 pm on Monday to Saturday. On Sunday it's 12 noon to

3 pm and 7 pm to 10.30 pm. The beers that you'll be able to choose from are Stones Bitter, Kimberley Best Bitter and Kimberley Classic, plus occasional guests. For food you can have a choice of a vegetarian menu (leek and mushroom crumble and broccoli and cheese pie for instance) plus traditional food such as lamb chops, deep fried plaice and steak and kidney pie – these are available from 12 noon until 2 pm every day and from 6.30 pm to 8.30 pm on Tuesday to Saturday. In summer meals are also available from 7 pm until 8 pm on a Sunday. Telephone: 01433 630415.

- **HOW TO GET THERE:** Calver can be found on the A623, approximately 1½ miles north of Baslow.
- **PARKING:** On the street or in the cul-de-sac in front of Curbar School.
- **LENGTH OF THE WALK:** 5¼ miles. Map: OS Outdoor Leisure 24 White Peak area (GR 248743).

THE WALK

1. From the layby in front of Curbar Primary School pass the Bridge Inn on the left. Then cross the bridge over the Derwent with Calver Mill on the right. Immediately over the bridge turn left on the tarmac path. With the river on your left pass under the A623 roadbridge. Continue beside the river with houses on your right. Continue downstream through a couple of fields before entering a wood. Follow the path through this, leaving the river behind. At the end of the wood climb the stile and continue along the obvious path and pass through a squeezer stile. Cross the field to a stile approximately 10 yards left of the gate in front of the wood ahead.

2. Turn left along the lane. Once again the Derwent is to your left as you enter Bubnell. Pass Bubnell Hall (on the right) then a weir to reach ancient Bubnell Bridge on the left. Our route passes through a stile on the right – opposite the bridge – but there are good views from both sides of the bridge so enjoy them. Pass through the stile mentioned above. After entering the first field walk forward with the wall on your right for three fields. Continue in a fourth field to reach the corner of a wall. Here turn right and then left – still in the same field beside the wall – to walk up to the top right corner. The view behind is worth enjoying. Continue forward in a fifth field up the right side to cross a stile. Then proceed alongside a thorn hedge

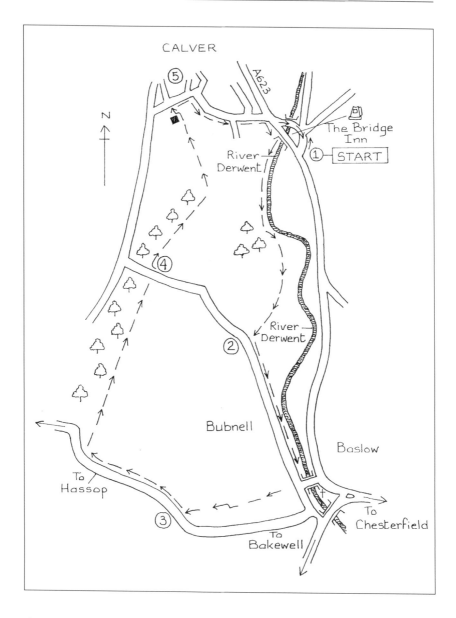

then a fence for 50 yards. From here the footpath bears half left to the top left hand corner of the field. However, people seem to walk straight forward here in the same direction as they've been walking before turning left at the end of the field to the gate in the corner.

3. This brings you to Wheatlands Lane. Turn right and continue for ¹/₂ mile. It rises initially until you reach the top with views of Longstone Edge ahead. Descend on the lane before it then levels out fairly quickly. On your right is a double gate. Take the stile beside this and walk alongside the wood on the left away from the road. Enter Bank Wood and keep on the ridgetop path for ³/₄ mile. Then cross a couple of steps leading over the wall on the right. Once over these turn left and follow the track to Bramley Lane.

4. Turn left along the lane for a few yards to enter Bramley Wood on the right. Stay on the clear path along the top of the wood for ¹/₂ mile. The path opens out. At the end of the ridge as the ground falls away walk forward, away from the corner of the wall. The obvious path you're on bends round to the left and downhill. Losing height fairly quickly, descend for 30 yards or so but instead of staying on the track you're on fork right down a path that descends fairly steeply towards the buildings on the left side of Calver. This section of path runs alongside a fence on the right. After crossing a stile keep forward to the valley bottom. Beyond this continue forward, bearing very slightly right towards the corner of a wall and fence 100 yards ahead. Walk forward with the wall on your right. Then cross the bottom of a narrow field to a stile with a house to the left. Cross this stile and (ignoring a path to the right after 10 yards) walk behind a double garage before turning left and then immediately right down a gravel drive between houses to a lane.

5. On the lane turn right. Ignore lanes to the left to reach a lamp in the middle of the road. Bear right into Main Street. Pass the Old Bulls Head (now a private house) and Calver Methodist Church, slowly losing height. Cross to the left hand side of the road and at Brook House you'll see a small brook incorporated in the gardens of four houses. Ignore a right turn into Brookfields and a left into Smithy Knoll Road. At the main road turn right. About 100 yards later take the road to the left signed 'Calver Mill'. Return to the start.

PLACES OF INTEREST NEARBY
Chatsworth House is just a few miles south where you can visit not just the house but also the gardens and the farm. Telephone: 01246 582204. At the far end of the park *Chatsworth Garden Centre* is popular with gardeners and visitors.

LINACRE RESERVOIRS

Linacre Reservoirs lie just outside the Peak District near Chesterfield, in an area that merits further visits. This lovely walk encircles all three reservoirs and takes in Old Brampton with its intriguing church clock.

A shady path near Linacre

Old Brampton marks the halfway point on this walk and is especially interesting because of the clock on the parish church of St Peter and St Paul. If you look carefully you will see there are 63 minutes marked. The story goes that the workman who was painting the clock face only got so far before he went for a drink at lunchtime. He came back rather the worse for wear and consequently painted a few too many minutes. The reservoirs are situated in a lovely wooded valley and provide the water for the town of Chesterfield.

The Three Merry Lads in Cutthorpe (telephone: 01246 277593) is a

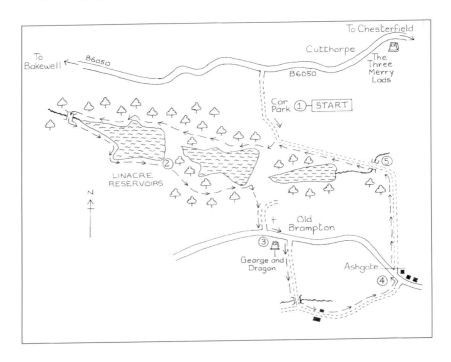

lively, friendly pub just down the road from Linacre Reservoirs, a little way off the walk route. It's open from 12 noon until 11 pm except on Sundays when it closes at 10.30 pm. A good choice of food is available from 12 noon until 8.30 pm every day, with (on Monday to Saturday) some excellent specials. Besides the usual favourites you can also enjoy dishes such as chicken fillet with white wine sauce or braised steak with onions. The beers are Mansfield Bitter, Riding and Redeye plus Woodpecker and Strongbow ciders.

- **HOW TO GET THERE:** Linacre Reservoirs can be reached from the B6050 west of Cutthorpe, 3½ miles from Chesterfield.
- **PARKING:** Approaching from Cutthorpe, turn left after leaving the village for Linacre Reservoirs. Park in the first car park/picnic site on the left along the access road.
- **LENGTH OF THE WALK:** 5 miles. Map: OS Outdoor Leisure 24 White Peak area (GR 336728).

THE WALK

1. From the car park turn left down the access road to the next car

On the path beside Upper Reservoir

park just over 100 yards downhill on the right. Bear slightly right across this and descend the wooden steps to reach a gravel track. Turn right downhill. Stay on this and walk towards Middle Reservoir ahead. Keep right of this, rising along the track. At Upper Reservoir (beyond the grassy embankment) keep right of this, following a path mostly near the water's edge to reach a wooden footbridge and later another (smaller) one. Continue to a third footbridge over Birley Brook at the top of the reservoir. Cross this and follow the path – again by the waterside. Part of this path runs along duckboarding – so keep your eye on the path! Continue on this path for some distance.

2. Pass the overflow from Upper Reservoir, ignoring a path to the left across the dam wall. Bear slightly right into the trees. This path takes you away from the reservoir. Ignore all detours to left and right. Stay on the main path. At the end of Middle Reservoir on your left pass through a gateway in the stone wall and bear right, soon descending but within a few yards rising again. Just 15 yards later take the right fork in the path then 5 or 6 yards after that take the sharp right turn up stone steps to cross a stone wall. Beyond this rise uphill with a wall on the left. Head forward to a farmgate in the far left corner. Pass over a stile beside this and turn right up the bridleway into Old Brampton.

3. Turn left at the road and pass the church, not forgetting to count the minutes on the clock! Continue past the George and Dragon to reach a tumbledown stone building on the right, 100 yards past the pub. Turn right and pass through the stone gateposts. Walk between hedgerows to cross a brook in the shallow valley bottom. Then rise slightly and turn left to pass Broomhall Farm with the farmhouse on the right. Just beyond this ignore a concrete track down to the left. Stay on the farm drive for 1/2 mile back to the road – ignore a track to the right for Leadhill Farm as you get near the road.

4. Enter Ashgate and turn left on the road. Some 100 yards later follow the bridleway to the right. Pass the entrance to Hadfield Barns and continue on this rough gravel track. About 1/2 mile later at a crossroads with a path to the left into a wood and a track to the right keep forward, passing Woodnook Cottage on the left. Continue on the bridleway between hedges. In the next wood ignore paths to left and right. As the bridleway rises into a clearing ignore a footbridge on the right.

5. Cross the stone bridge over the brook. Rise steadily uphill. Just beyond the toilet block on the right keep on the tarmac access road (ignoring all left forks) all the way back to the car park.

PLACES OF INTEREST NEARBY
Just to the north-east, in Old Whittington, is *Revolution House*. Now a fascinating museum, it was here in the 17th century that three members of the local gentry plotted against King James II. Telephone: 01246 453554.

CHESTERFIELD AND THE CHESTERFIELD CANAL

This walk is a revelation – don't miss it – you will be surprised how attractive the canal is. The volunteers who have been restoring it should be praised to the sky. Look out for kingfishers as well as other waterlife.

The Chesterfield Canal

Chesterfield's crooked spire must be one of the most unusual architectural features in England. Topping the church of St Mary and All Saints, the spire appears from some angles to be nearly vertical. This curiosity occurred quite by accident and not only does it lean but it has twisted as well. This is due to green timbers being used in centuries long gone.

The canal was constructed at the end of the 18th century and linked Chesterfield with the Trent at West Stockwith 46 miles away.

It had 65 locks and two tunnels – the collapse of one of these being the main reason for its fall into disuse. The remains of the canal can be followed as the Cuckoo Way and this makes an enjoyable waterside walk for at least some of its length. Sadly a stretch of the disused canal has been built on at Killamarsh so as the Chesterfield Canal Society hope one day to complete the restoration of the canal there may have to be some re-routing!

The Donkey Derby, across the A61, not far from the walk's starting point, is a brand new pub with no history – it's not been going long enough. Traditionalists tend to frown on new pubs but this is nonsense – a pub is a pub is a pub. It's open all day, the staff are helpful and friendly and food is always available. Interesting dishes like tuna pasta bake, Mexican chicken and fisherman's catch crumble are available as well as a children's menu. There are vegetarian meals too – roasted red pepper lasagne being one that caught my eye. Stones, Boddingtons and Directors Bitter are available, with two guest beers. The ciders include Scrumpy Jack and Woodpecker. Telephone: 01246 554485.

- **HOW TO GET THERE:** You should be able to find Chesterfield quite easily – finding Tapton Lock Visitor Centre needs a little more care. Get there by taking the A61 north from Chesterfield. At the A619 (Worksop) roundabout turn into Lockoford Lane, also signed 'Canal Lock'. Lockoford Lane is between the A61 and the A619 on the roundabout. To visit the Donkey Derby pub take the road signed 'Stonegravels and Newbold' on this roundabout.
- **PARKING:** Park on the road beside the Tapton Lock Visitor Centre.
- **LENGTH OF THE WALK:** 5½ miles. Maps: OS Pathfinders 761 Chesterfield and 762 Worksop (South) and Staveley (GR 387729).

THE WALK
1. Descend to the canal, signed 'Cuckoo Way – Chesterfield 1 mile'. Walk on the right side of the canal, passing the Visitor Centre on the far side. A sign points one way to Chesterfield and the other to Istanbul. The canal is part of the Trans-Pennine Trail. Pass through Tapton Tunnel 1A. Below to the right is the River Rother. Eventually you arrive at the attractive redbrick Tapton Mill Bridge with the crooked spire in the background. Cross the bridge and continue with the canal on your right. Avoid a path rising uphill to the left – stay by the canal. Cross a metal footbridge and keep to the towpath.

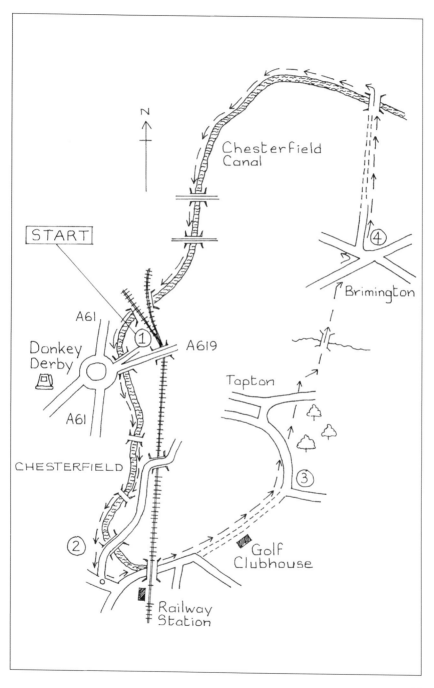

N

Chesterfield Canal

START

A61

Donkey Derby

A61

A619

CHESTERFIELD

②

Tapton

Brimington

④

③

Golf Clubhouse

Railway Station

Bluebank Lock

The crooked spire draws nearer. At a pavement beside a road turn left to the main road.

2. Turn right towards the crooked spire, keeping the Trebor Bassett factory on your right. Turn left at the roundabout. Some 50 yards later turn left again towards the railway station. Stay on the road to the left of the station – this is signed 'Tapton Golf Course ½ mile'. Pass under two railway bridges. Take care here. Keep on the road as it rises. Behind is a good view of the crooked spire. Ignore a road to the right. Continue ascending to fork left off the road into Tapton Park. Follow the driveway towards the clubhouse. At the entrance bear left, descending gently, with the clubhouse 50 yards to the right. At the end of the brick wall on the right keep forward on the track, descending into a hollow. Follow the track as it bears right then left to rise uphill between a hedge on the left and conifers on the right. Keep ascending with the golf course on both sides. The track brings you to a narrow country lane.

3. Turn left on this for 300 yards. At the end of a wood on the right turn right through a gateway. Walk down the field beside the wood towards Tapton Hall Farm. Ignore the cross-path halfway down the field. Keep forward down the right side of the farm. Cross a narrow lane. Beyond, walk down the right side of a short field, then bear right for 75 yards. At the end of the woodland on the left pass through a gateway and walk diagonally across the field in front. This leads in the general direction of Brimington on the hillside ahead – the path you're following should be heading 40 yards left of the bottom right corner of the field! Once over the bridge keep in the same direction towards a farmgate 300 yards ahead on the right side of the field. Continue into the hedged track. Keep forward to the main road in Brimington, ignoring a path on the right as you go. Turn right at the main road and then cross to the far side. About ¼ mile later turn left down Devonshire Street.

4. At the mini-roundabout walk along Coronation Road. Stay on this, avoiding roads to each side. Ignore the cul-de-sac sign at the end of the road – this applies to cars. Continue as the road becomes a bridleroad, leaving the houses behind. Ignore a driveway to the left after 250 yards and a track to the right after another 250 yards. At the canal cross this and turn left. The walk back to the start is a surprise and delight just 2 miles from the centre of Chesterfield. Pass Bluebank Lock. Moorhens, swans and coots abound. Cross a couple of roads but stay beside the canal to reach Brimington Wharf. Pass under two railway bridges. Later pass under a roadbridge to arrive back at the Tapton Lock Visitor Centre.

PLACES OF INTEREST NEARBY

Visit *St Mary and All Saints church* (the Crooked Spire to give it its more commonly known name) which is open all year. Access to the Spire itself is however only possible most Bank Holiday Mondays and other (advertised) times. Or visit the *Chesterfield Museum and Art Gallery* in St Mary's Gate. Telephone: 01246 345727.

MONYASH AND THE
RIVER LATHKILL

᪨᪨᪨

Truly impressive Peak District scenery in a deservedly popular area.
The longer route will take you away from the busier paths for a while.

Tufa Waterfall

For 200 years from the end of the 17th century to the end of the
19th century Monyash was something of a Quaker stronghold with
One Ash Grange, the home of the Bowman family, being a
particular focus. When the Bowmans 'removed' (as they put it) from
Leek in Staffordshire to Monyash in 1697 One Ash Grange was the
actual meeting house for local Quakers. It was only later that the
small Meeting House near the car park in Monyash was built.
Behind the old Meeting House are some of the simple Quaker
tombstones. The farm where the Bowmans lived, passed on the
walk, was owned by the Duke of Devonshire and the only reason

the Bowmans left was that the then Duke intended to raise the rent by 10%. This the Bowmans could not or would not pay. So after 200 years they left One Ash though it still attracts descendants of the family back from time to time.

Lathkill Dale itself forms part of English Nature's Derbyshire Reserve. The top end of the River Lathkill tends to dry up during the summer in particular and at other dry times. This is partly due to the porous nature of the limestone. Swallow-holes have been created over the centuries by water erosion so the rivers in this area in many cases now flow underground. It's only at times of heavy rain that they reappear. You may have to travel quite a way down the dale (I nearly wrote downstream which is wholly inappropriate if you have no river) before you find the Lathkill flowing on the surface.

Being the only pub in a village sometimes means that it sits back on its heels – but not the Bull's Head in Monyash. The beer is good and so is the food. It's a very popular pub with visitors and on summer days they're even lying outside on the green. The opening times are from 12 noon to 3 pm and from 7 pm to 11 pm every day. Food can be purchased from 12 noon until 2 pm during the week and until 2.30 pm at the weekend. In the evening food is available from 7 pm until 9 pm (weekdays) or 9.30 pm (weekends). Tetley Bitter and Mild plus Ind Coope Burton Ale and a guest which changes regularly are also on offer. If you like cider you've got a choice between Woodpecker and Strongbow. For a time the pub used to be known as the Hobbit but reverted to the Bull's Head which seems much more in keeping with this attractive Derbyshire village. Telephone: 01629 812372.

- **HOW TO GET THERE:** Monyash is 5 miles west of Bakewell on the B5055.
- **PARKING:** Turn off the B5055 northwards at the crossroads in Monyash to reach the small car park, 100 yards away.
- **LENGTH OF THE WALK:** 5³/₄ miles, or a shorter route of 4 miles which omits the second stretch along Lathkill Dale. Map: OS Outdoor Leisure 24 White Peak area (GR 150667).

THE WALK

1. From the car park turn left on the road away from the Bull's Head. Immediately beyond Melbourne House is the old Quaker Meeting House and behind it the small cemetery. Continue along the

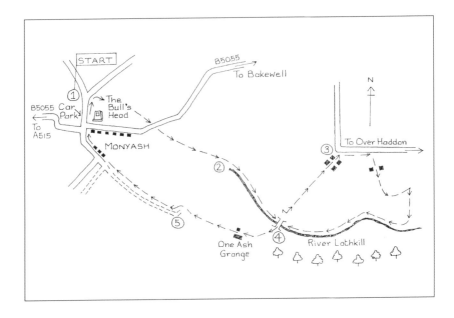

road. At the bottom of the slope turn right onto the Sheldon road. Immediately beyond the garden on the right pass through a stile. Follow the obvious path through Bagshaw Dale. Keep in the bottom of the dale. A few yards before the road keep left of the stone building to climb a stile onto the road. Turn left towards the toilet block – the plaque on the side may raise a wry smile. Enter the field immediately past the toilet. Follow the path through the bottom of the field and enter the Lathkill Dale National Nature Reserve. Follow the obvious path. Cross a stile into the dale proper where the terrain is rockier. Continue to descend to reach Ricklow Quarry with a large spoil heap on the left and awkward rocks underfoot. Stay on the path further into the dale to arrive at a low cave on the right.

2. This is where the River Lathkill starts – sometimes. Continue past it to come to a wooden footbridge. Turn right here for the short walk (go to point 4 below). The longer walk turns sharp left (uphill) at this point. Follow the path as it zigzags quite steeply to a marvellous view at the top. Enter the field through a gate. Keep forward away from the dale, parallel to the wall on the right. Climb over the stile 15 or 20 yards to the right of a gateway. In the second field walk parallel to the wall on the left. Pass through the narrow

Lathkill Dale, near Ricklow Quarry

wood ahead. Bear very slightly right towards the farm. Stay on the left side of the barn and walk forward through the farmyard to the road.

3. Turn right here for 325 yards. Turn right down the drive to Mill Farm. At the end of the straight driveway fork left between the farm buildings. Keep forward over a stile into a walled lane. Follow this as it descends into the (unnamed) dale. Zigzag down the track into the valley bottom. This path is not overused and is much quieter than Lathkill Dale itself. At the bottom of the dale (hopefully the river is running) turn right upstream back to the wooden footbridge referred to above.

4. Cross this and follow the path as it bears left. Look behind to see the zigzag path which takes the longer route up the side of the dale. The path you're on leads into Cales Dale. Ignore a path descending to the left. Stay on the path to rise up the right side of this dry dale. This brings you to a small limestone tor. The path then rises upwards into a field. From the stile walk ahead towards the farm. The path leads to some 'steps' immediately to the left of the barn.

41

Walk alongside this and keep forward at the end to pass an old icehouse on the right and an old toilet on the left. Just beyond pass the pig sties on the right. With the camping barn on the left look to the apex of the building on the right. There are some initials to be seen – C.B. and A.B. and a date, '1700'. These refer to Cornelius and Anne Bowman (the author's great-great-great-great-great-great-great-grandparents). From this point, turn right up the track. Ignore a concessionary path forking left. Continue up the straight track for 200 yards, leaving the farm behind. Pass through a farmgate on the right at the top of the track. Turn left immediately beyond the gate and walk alongside the wall for 450 yards. At the end of the field cross the stile on the left. Once over this turn right and continue in the same direction as before to negotiate two more stiles. Then walk slightly uphill to the far right corner of the next field. Climb this and turn left to a walled path 25 yards away.

5. Follow this for ¹/₂ mile to the outskirts of Monyash. Ignore a driveway on the left. As you join the road keep straight ahead into the village. Pass Fere Mere on the right with the church beyond. This is one of the places where the villagers used to get their water – it doesn't look very appetising now. (Just beyond is an unusual stile in the garden wall opposite the mere.) Continue forward to reach the green in front of the Bull's Head and the car park.

PLACES OF INTEREST NEARBY
Head 7 miles north-west and visit *Buxton* with its impressive Opera House and the Crescent. Or drive south-west and enjoy some spectacular scenery around *Crowdecote* and *Longnor*.

YOULGREAVE: BESIDE THE RIVERS
LATHKILL AND BRADFORD

Two of Derbyshire's loveliest dales are featured in this walk – Lathkill and Bradford – enjoy them. In some parts of Lathkill Dale above Conksbury Bridge the colour of the water is almost turquoise.

A packhorse bridge near Youlgreave

Like so many other Derbyshire villages, Youlgreave has hardly any houses that match each other. They are all different and this adds character to the place. The well dressings which take place at Midsummer, near St John the Baptist's Day, are very popular with both locals and visitors. Telephone the Tourist Information Centre in Bakewell (01629 813227) for more details.

The Bull's Head (in the centre of Youlgreave) is a family run pub with a ghost called George who smells of candlewax. As you can imagine it's a pub with character. There's a choice of beers – Marston's Pedigree, Bitter and Smooth – plus Strongbow cider. The

43

food includes good traditional items such as various steaks, cod, plaice and scampi and steak pie as well as one or two dishes originating from further afield such as lasagne verdi. Food is served from 12 noon to 2 pm and 7.30 pm to 9 pm every day. The pub is actually open from 11.30 am to 2 pm and 6.30 pm to 11 pm during the week, 11.30 am to 11 pm on Saturday and 12 noon until 10.30 pm on Sunday. Telephone: 01629 636307.

- **HOW TO GET THERE:** Youlgreave is 3 miles south of Bakewell.
- **PARKING:** Park in the small car park at the western end of the village – this is also its highest point. Youlgreave can be very busy at weekends so bear this in mind. To reach the Bull's Head walk down the main street towards the church. The pub is on the right.
- **LENGTH OF THE WALK:** 6¹/₄ miles. Map: OS Outdoor Leisure 24 White Peak area (GR 205641).

THE WALK

1. From the car park walk down the road towards the centre of the village. At the Old Hall on the left fork right at the Wesleyan Reform Church then immediately left at Brookleton. Descend the road, then the tarmac path with Dale View on the right. Follow the path down to the River Bradford. Turn left at the bottom. Walk to the road. Continue forward to a gateway and walk on the track beyond with the river on your right. The track crosses this after a few yards. Continue downstream. Pass a small packhorse bridge. Where the track bears right uphill take the stile by the small gate. Follow the path to the roadside in the hamlet of Alport.

2. (If you would like a short detour here to see this attractive hamlet turn right down the lane and then keep left until you return to this spot.) Cross the road. Follow the obvious path through the fields with the River Lathkill to the right to reach a narrow lane by Raper Lodge. (Turn right to see lovely Raper Bridge a few yards away. There are often fish waiting to be fed underneath.) Cross this lane and continue along the clear path, later bearing right to reach the road. Turn right to Conksbury Bridge. Cross this roadbridge and turn left along the path up the right side of the river. The water in the river higher up on this section can be amazingly clear and visitors are asked not to swim here. Continue to Lathkill Lodge – the white house in the bottom of the dale.

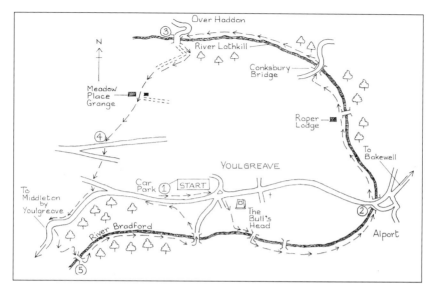

3. Cross the river to the left, assuming there is any water in it. It can disappear underground during dry spells. On the far side turn left uphill and subsequently right to the field above. Pass through the farmgate and enjoy the view of Over Haddon across the valley. This is where the Wildgoose family lived in the 19th century and earlier. They were farmers and leadminers. From here walk across the field to the farm buildings of Meadow Place Grange – originally owned by monks and used as a sheep farm. Pass through a pair of gates (one after the other) leading into the farmyard. Cross this to the gate directly opposite. Climb the step stile beside the gate. Continue forward away from the farmyard and follow the signpost for Middleton Moor Lane. This leads alongside the high wall on the right. Do not follow the wall all the way round though – bear slightly left away from it along the fairly obvious path. This rises to a stile. Once through this keep in a straight line towards the far corner of the next field. Climb the stile and keep in the same direction towards the wood ahead. This brings you to a lane.

4. Cross this and continue through the field beyond. Pass through the narrow wood and head to the gate across the field with Moor Lane beyond. Cross this and pass through a small gap stile. Walk on the left side of the first three fields. Keep right of a gateway after 20 yards in the fourth field and keep forward to a squeezer stile just

The River Lathkill, below Over Haddon

beyond a dewpond. Pass through the remaining stiles to the road. Cross the road into the field on the other side. Descend to the gate at the bottom of the field. Turn right along the road for 450 yards. At the sharp left hand bend cross the stile on the left and descend the path which is part of the Limestone Way.

5. Cross the bridge over the river and turn left down the dale. The river hereabouts can dry up almost completely in summer. Continue until you reach an old clapper bridge on the left. Cross this and, with Manor House Tearooms ahead of you, turn immediately left once you're over the bridge. Follow the tarmac path uphill between the cottages. Continue up the path, ignoring a path to the left. When you reach an open area in front of Chapel Cottages take the path to the left of these. At the main street opposite the Primitive Methodist Chapel turn left back to the car park – or right to the Bull's Head!

PLACES OF INTEREST NEARBY

Caudwells Mill in Rowsley, 4 miles north-east, is open to the public and has a number of craft shops as well as the excellent Country Parlour where delicious food is available. The Mill itself is also open to the public and you can even buy some flour that has been ground on the premises. Telephone: 01629 734374.

WALK 10

DARLEY BRIDGE AND LADYGROVE

*On this walk you will visit the three dams at Ladygrove, which
extends north-east from Two Dales. If you enjoy walking in tree-
lined valleys you will want to come back time and again to this
lovely and little-known area.*

Nancy Dam

Darley Dale, the town which includes Darley Bridge, where the walk
starts, South Darley and Two Dales (or Toadhole as it was known),
straddles the A6, lying largely within the Derwent Valley between
Rowsley and Matlock. There were two great influences on life in
Darley Dale: the Railway and Sir Joseph Whitworth. A manufacturer
and benefactor in the 19th century, Sir Joseph founded the local
Whitworth Hospital, the Whitworth Institute, now used as a
community centre and Whitworth Park.

But the influence of the railway was such that even the town's
name was their creation. In around 1890 the attractive 'Dale' was

47

added to the original name of their station — Darley. Now, after many years' absence, steam trains can be seen again in Darley Dale, courtesy of Peak Rail, a group of railway enthusiasts. On the walk you have an opportunity to see the steam engines at close quarters. The steam engines chugging up the line each weekend are a splendid sight.

The Square and Compass pub, at the north end of Darley Bridge, dates from 1735 although there's evidence that there's been a brewhouse here for 700 years or more. There's a wide choice of dishes from the usual (scampi, ocean pie, lasagne, sirloin steak) to the more exotic (sizzling ostrich steak and chicken rigatoni). The beers are Robinson's Best Bitter and Frederic's Premium Bitter, Guinness and Carling Black Label plus Scrumpy Jack and Strongbow ciders. Opening times are from 12 noon to 3 pm and 5.30 pm to 11 pm (7 pm to 10.30 pm on Sunday evening). Food is served from 12 noon to 2 pm and 5.30 pm to 9 pm (7 pm to 9 pm on Sunday evening).

- **HOW TO GET THERE:** Darley Bridge is 2½ miles north-west of Matlock. Follow the B5057 off the A6 in Darley Dale and continue over the railway and the crossroads to a left hand bend with a picnic site on the right next to the cricket ground.
- **PARKING:** You can park at the picnic site or in the pub car park opposite the Square and Compass a little further on.
- **LENGTH OF THE WALK:** 5 miles. Map: OS Outdoor Leisure 24 White Peak area (GR 270623).

THE WALK

1. From the picnic site turn right on the road past the Square and Compass. Where the road bends right keep forward. Pass through the right hand stile and walk along the track on the left side of the farm buildings. Pass through a pair of stiles with the farmhouse on the right. Continue alongside the wall. Pass through two more stiles. Cross the middle of the third field to reach the River Derwent. Riber Castle stands on the hillside further down the valley. Cross the stone bridge over Warney Brook. Walk forward and cross the railway line. Climb the steps beyond. Continue on the path with the Red House Hotel over the wall on the left.

2. At the end of the buildings turn right on the gravel track and

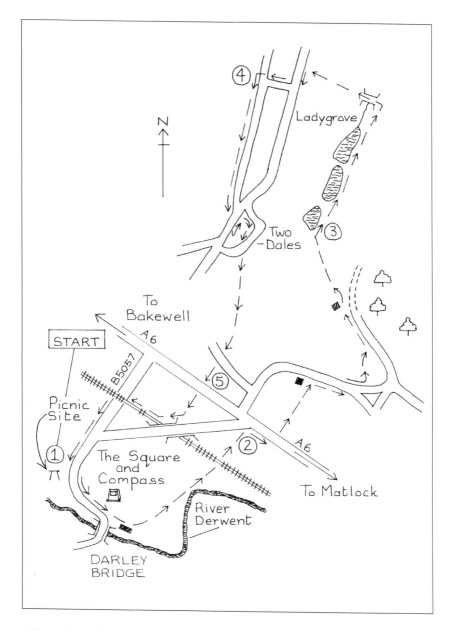

follow it to the A6. Cross carefully here and turn right for 100 yards. Opposite Rotherwood turn left into the grounds of St Elphin's School. Bear very slightly left off the driveway. Head just left of the

One of the small waterfalls in Ladygrove

brick buildings ahead. Pass through a kissing gate and walk up the right side of the field. Do not follow the hedge as it bears right – keep forward to the fence corner two-thirds of the way up the field. Pass through the stile just beyond the corner. Keep in the same direction as before, walking up the left side of the field to the road. Turn right for 250 yards. Ignore Blind Lane. Just beyond turn left opposite house number 32 and follow the tarmac track uphill. This narrows to a path bringing you to Holt Road. Keep forward, bearing slightly left. Walk below the bungalows on the top side of the lane. Pass Sharder Well. Continue to a cottage on the left – fork left down the narrow path.

3. At the bottom turn right along a roughish track to enter Ladygrove. Pass the first dam on the left – Nancy Dam. Later ignore a track turning sharp right to continue with Fancy Dam far below on the left. Keep forward high above the third dam, Potter Dam, below to the left. The path is crossed here and there by small watercourses and there are even one or two miniature waterfalls. At the end of the third and last dam Sydnope Brook lies below. At the end of the path (with a waterfall to the left – assuming it's running!)

rise up the banking to the right. Walk beside a tumbled down wall on the left and keep beside this – ignore a path forking right into the trees. Continue alongside the wall to reach a path descending from the right. Turn left downhill to a bridge over Sydnope Brook. Cross this. Walk up to a stile at the top of the field. Turn round and admire the view of the woodland behind. In the next field walk forward, bearing very slightly right towards the group of buildings ahead – aim just to the left of a pair of electricity poles. Beyond these walk up the right side of the garden of Sydnope Hall Farm to the road. Turn left for 150 yards then right up a tarmac lane.

4. Where the lane turns right, turn left down the gravel track and stay on this for ½ mile. Halldale is away to your right. At the road turn right downhill for 50 yards. Pass through the stile by the farmgate into the field on the left. Fork left after a few yards into the trees. Stay on this path to reach a narrow back lane. Turn right, ignore Knabb Lane and continue downhill to join another road from the left. Turn right for 150 yards then left immediately beyond Holt House. This is signed for 'Oddford Lane'. Follow the track to a stile on a crossroads of paths. Keep forward into the field beyond, bearing slightly right – keep left of the tree in the middle of the field. Pass through a stile and walk towards the gateway beyond. Before the gate turn right on the tarmac path and follow this to the narrow lane. Cross this and follow the path to the A6.

5. Cross this carefully and walk along the left side of the field beyond. Then cross the stile and old bridge to walk on the left side of the next field between two fences. At the road turn right for 30 yards, cross the entrance to DFS and turn right down some steps. Follow the path alongside the railway line to reach Station Road and the Peak Rail station. At the road turn left, keep straight on at the crossroads and return to the picnic site.

PLACES OF INTEREST NEARBY
Visit *Peak Rail* itself and perhaps have a ride on one of the steam trains. You could also visit the *Red House Stables* whose horses and carriages have been featured in very many period TV series. To reach the stables return to the crossroads between the picnic site and Peak Rail and turn right – the stables are ½ mile further on. Telephone: 01629 733583.

WALK 11
OGSTON RESERVOIR

Take your binoculars when you make a circuit of this delightful reservoir. There are often many wildfowl to see.

Ogston Reservoir

Ogston Reservoir was built in the late 1950s at the top of the Amber Valley and has a sailing club as well as being popular with birdwatchers. The walk does not pass through any villages as such although it will take you past a number of interesting houses near Brackenfield Green. It's worth looking out for glimpses of Ogston Hall through the trees at the far end of the reservoir and the mill leet near Ogston Bridge. This runs between the river and the railway line to the old mill further down the valley.

The New Napoleon, located on the road that runs along the north side of the reservoir, is a rather charming pub. The food is interesting and very tasty, for example monkfish, mussel and prawn fricassee in a creamy mushroom sauce. There are less exotic sounding dishes, though, if you want something a bit plainer –

52

perhaps home-made meat and potato pie or grilled fillet of Ogston trout. There's an excellent choice of real ales too with Boddingtons, Flowers Original, Wadworth 6X, Castle Eden and sometimes Stones and Tetley as guests – plus Strongbow for the cider lover. The pub is closed on a Monday but otherwise is open from 12 noon to 2.30 pm and 6 pm to 11 pm every day. Food is available (except Mondays) from 12 noon to 2 pm and 6 pm to 9.30 pm. Telephone: 01246 590413.

- **HOW TO GET THERE:** Ogston Reservoir is 6½ miles south of Chesterfield and 5 miles east of Matlock. Just south of Clay Cross follow the B6014 westwards from the A61 for 1¼ miles to reach a picnic site on the left just after Boar Farm on the right. The New Napoleon is 300 yards later on the right.
- **PARKING:** You can park at the picnic site – please do not leave your car at the pub until you visit it for a meal or drink.
- **LENGTH OF THE WALK:** 5 miles. Map: OS Pathfinder 761 Chesterfield and 794 Crich and Bullbridge (GR 375610).

THE WALK

1. From the picnic site turn right along the road and take care. Pass Boar Farm. As the road rises uphill and bends left turn right along the tarmac bridleway. This gives good views of the reservoir. Stay on this lane for ³⁄₄ mile, passing Castle Farm and South Hill Farm. The reservoir isn't always visible because of trees. At the end of the water follow the road as it bears left for 275 yards, passing Ford Farm Barn then a high stone wall on the right. At the T-junction turn sharp right through Ogston Treatment Plant. Walk forward with the grassy dam wall to the right. Cross a bridge over the River Amber – the 'private' sign relates to motorists not walkers. At a T-junction turn left along a roughish track – the other way leads to Ogston Hall. Proceed towards a ridge of high ground. Along this runs Ryknild Street – a Roman road still in use in some places.

2. Turn right immediately after crossing Ogston Bridge. Follow the Amber for 15 yards then walk forward on the clear path as the river flows away to the right. Away to the left is the railway line, out of sight initially. After a while a footbridge over the railway line will be visible – to the right of it is the footbridge you need to cross over the river. Don't head towards the railway line – keep forward with

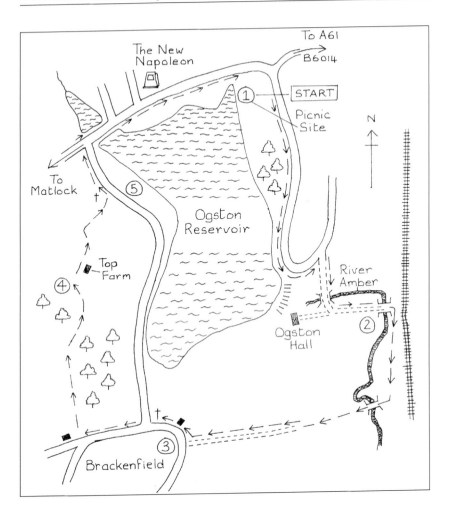

the river 20 or 30 yards to the right. Cross the footbridge over the river and turn right (with the river on your right) to double electricity posts 20 yards away. Walk past these. Keep on in the same direction towards a single post with a stile just beyond. Keep straight ahead in the next field towards a hedge corner. At the hedge corner is a path between hedges leading slightly uphill. It then runs along the left side of a small wood for 100 yards. Continue to the lane 300 yards later.

3. At the lane turn right for 350 yards to reach Brackenfield church.

54

(If you wish you can turn right here along the road to reach disused Woolley Methodist Chapel – and continue from point 5 below. This will shorten the walk and keep you nearer the reservoir.) The full route continues uphill for 400 yards on the Tansley and Matlock road. Turn right between Nether Farm and Holly Cottage. Follow this hedged path with glimpses of the reservoir on the right. Walk on the bottom side of the first field you reach. Then cross the narrow strip of rough ground. Keep on the bottom side of the next field (with Ogston Carr wood on your right). At the end of the wood keep forward beside the hedge on the right. Pass through a squeezer stile and walk to a stile to the left of the farmgate ahead. Beyond this keep forward in the next two fields to reach the corner of the wood ahead. Walk alongside this, bearing left at the end of the field to pass through a stile on the right leading down into a shallow, wooded valley. In the field beyond bear slightly right across the field. In the next field turn right downhill for 150 yards to Carr Brook. Cross a bridge and walk up the right side of the field ahead – as you go the path rises uphill and bears left. Some 200 yards later pass through a squeezer stile into another field.

4. Turn right with the hedge on your right. Pass through a farmgate and walk on the left side of the next field to a gate leading into the farmyard. Walk forward, keeping all farm buildings on your right, to reach the farm drive. Walk on this away from the farm and 100 yards later pass through the first gate (a double gate) on the left. Walk on the right side of the field beyond for 75 yards. Cross a stile beside a gate. Turn right along a walled path and 100 yards later pass through a stile on the left into the field below. Head slightly right to the wall jutting into the field. When you reach this bear left to the old chapel at the roadside. This is Woolley Methodist Chapel – long unused. Turn left.

5. Continue along the lane then turn right at the T-junction. This takes you across the reservoir. Ignore two left turns, pass the New Napoleon and return to the picnic site – taking care as you go.

PLACES OF INTEREST NEARBY
Drive 7 miles eastwards to *Hardwick Hall* (NT) (telephone: 01246 850430) or 5 miles south to *Crich Tramway Museum* (telephone: 01773 852565).

THORPE AND THE RIVER DOVE

The path through Dovedale is probably the busiest in Derbyshire –
especially on a Sunday. Why is this? The stunning scenery of course.
If you want to get away from the crowds walk it midweek or on a
Saturday – or try the evening in summer.

The raised path in Dovedale

Nestling just inside the boundary with Staffordshire, Thorpe is an
attractive village with an interesting church. The view from here
towards the Staffordshire village of Ilam (pronounced 'Eye-lam') is
quite breathtaking. There are many other lovely views to be had too
and Dovedale is always a delight.

The Dog and Partridge, just to the east of Thorpe, is a popular
port of call for walkers who fancy a drink after enjoying the
Derbyshire air. It is open (and food is available) from 12 noon until
9ish 'in season' – though it may stay open a bit longer than this. Out
of season the pub may be closed between 3pm and 5.30pm. They

tend to be flexible depending on who's about and the weather. Bass and Pedigree are available plus Strongbow cider and Guinness. The food is a mix of dishes from a sandwich to a steak to a vegetarian meal and includes items such as butterfly chicken breast, steak and kidney pie and lamb chump steak. Telephone: 01335 350235.

- **HOW TO GET THERE:** Thorpe is 3 miles north-west of Ashbourne, off the A515.
- **PARKING:** Park in the Narlow Lane car park opposite the Dog and Partridge or the pub car park if you are a customer.
- **LENGTH OF THE WALK:** 6¹/₄ miles. Map: OS Outdoor Leisure 24 White Peak area (GR 163505).

THE WALK

1. Face the front of the pub. Turn right up the single track lane. Proceed up this, passing Pike House, and enter Thorpe Pastures, owned by the National Trust. There are wide views from here. Continue along the lane for 300 yards after leaving the National Trust property to reach a stile on the left (and one on the right). Take the left one. Follow the track. About 100 yards after it has run alongside a wall on the right, climb the stile in the wall. Cross the corner of the field to the open gateway 50 yards away. In the third field from the road head just left of the highest group of trees ahead. Walk to the far left corner of the fourth field. In the field beyond proceed beside a wall on the left into a sixth field where the trees are now on the left. Keep parallel to the woodland to enter a narrow field with an impressive limekiln to the left. Walk directly across this field to the stile ahead. Keep in the same general direction as before. Bear slightly left as an attractive view of the dales ahead opens up. As you proceed there should be a wall corner 60 yards away to your right with a clump of trees beyond. Keep on to the stile ahead. Cross this and walk to the wall corner in front. Cross the stile here with a rocky mound to the right. Continue along the bottom side of this field towards Bostern Grange Farm.

2. Pass through the stile by the farmgate at the end of the wall. Walk forward on the drive past the farm buildings on the left. At the end of the buildings, after passing through a gateway, turn immediately left alongside the buildings. Then continue alongside a line of trees. Cross the stile in the field corner. Continue alongside a wall on the

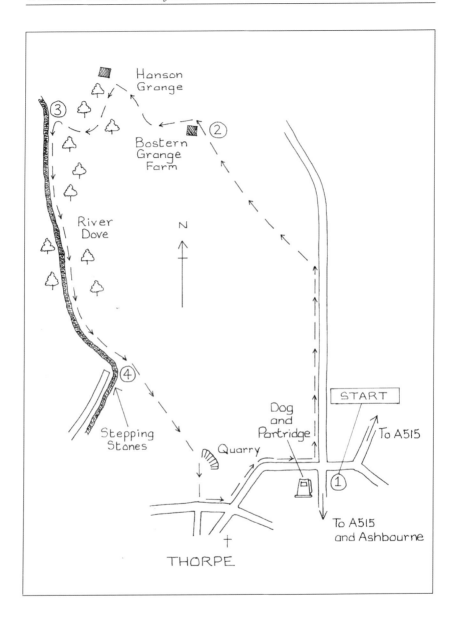

left. Another marvellous view begins to open out now. In the bottom left corner of this field cross the stile and immediately turn right over another stile. Walk alongside the wall on the right towards Hanson Grange ahead. Cross the stile at the end of the wall. Bear

Ilam Rock

slightly left towards the track leading to the Grange. Just before it enters the farmyard turn sharp left down the slope to pass through a stile into Nabs Dale – another National Trust property. Follow the path as it descends for $3/4$ mile into Dovedale.

3. Turn left with the beautiful River Dove on the right. Almost immediately you pass a couple of largish caves known as Dove Holes. Climbers can often be seen hanging upside down from the roof of these caves. About $1/3$ mile later you reach Ilam Rock with an elegant footbridge in front of it. Just 30 yards past this is Lion's Head Rock jutting out above and to the left of the path. As you proceed you will pass some impressive examples of path construction due to erosion caused by the hordes of walkers who pour into Dovedale each week – including you. Reynard's Cave is tucked up sharp left about $1/2$ mile past Ilam Rock and can be easily missed. Then almost immediately beyond a small brick pumping station on the left are the limestone columns of Tissington Spires which rise high above. The dale eventually opens out and the path bears right to pass through a stile down to the famous stepping stones with Thorpe Cloud rising high above to the left of these.

4. Our route doesn't quite reach the stepping stones though. Once you've passed through one of a pair of squeezer stiles turn left and go through the kissing gate to walk up Lin Dale with Thorpe Cloud rising above on the right. Initially the path runs up a gravel track before it becomes a wide grassy path – then a gravel track again. Where the fence/tumbled down wall bears right by a hollow in the ground keep forward, bearing very slightly right to pick up and follow a shallow hollow way 50 yards or so to the right of a rocky outcrop. With a small quarry on the left proceed towards the tower of Thorpe church in the distance. Follow the grassy track away from the quarry to enter the Wintercroft Lane car park. Turn left on the road and follow it all the way back to the start $1/2$ mile later, ignoring roads to left and right.

PLACES OF INTEREST NEARBY
Ilam Hall, a National Trust property, is just a couple of miles to the west (telephone: 01335 350245). You could also visit *Ashbourne* with its impressive church and attractive shops.

WALK 13
CARSINGTON WATER

A stroll to the attractive village of Kirk Ireton, then a bracing walk on the eastern side of the reservoir. This is a most enjoyable circuit with some excellent views.

Carsington Water

The reservoir known as Carsington Water was opened early in the 1990s and has proved to be quite a 'honeypot'. Visitors have the opportunity to cycle, sail dinghies and sailboards, fish and watch birds. The Barrowdale Restaurant at the Visitor Centre is open from 10 am until 5.45 pm and there's a good range of food from home-made soup, gammon, chicken curry with rice or jacket potatoes, salads and toasties. There are also scones, toasties and cakes. The restaurant can get very busy on Sundays and bank holidays. Telephone: 01629 540363.

Kirk Ireton, the village passed through early in the walk, provides a contrast. Here the Barley Mow is a traditional pub in the best

61

traditions! There's no piped music or slot machines and the bar is a very simple affair. If it's open, it is well worth a visit as you pass through the village. It really is a pub you will remember for a long time. Telephone: 01335 370306.

- **HOW TO GET THERE:** Carsington Reservoir is 3 miles south-west of Wirksworth. Follow the signs for the reservoir from the A5035 Wirksworth–Ashbourne road. Pass the Visitor Centre on the left and continue below the grassy reservoir embankment to the Millfields car park on the far side of the reservoir.
- **PARKING:** For the walk, park in the Millfields car park. At present tickets bought there can also be used at the Visitor Centre car park.
- **LENGTH OF THE WALK:** 7$^1/_4$ miles. Map: OS Outdoor Leisure 24 White Peak area with Pathfinder 811 Belper for the beginning and end of the walk (GR 248498).

THE WALK

1. Find a space in the car park near the water's edge. With the reservoir on your left and the toilet block on your right walk through the car park. Take the path veering left slightly downhill – this is the closest path to the water. About 20 to 30 yards later enter a copse of trees. Cross the wooden footbridge. On joining another path bear left, following the 'walking' route beside the reservoir. This clear gravel path brings you to a tarmac lane (Hays Lane). Turn right uphill. Ignore a footpath on the right. Pass the entrance to Riddings Farm. At the top cross the lane running from left to right. Walk forward through the field in the same direction as before. Then cross a narrow field to the stile opposite. In the third field bear very slightly right to pass through a gap in the hedge ahead. Keep forward in the fourth field and pass through another gap in a hedge. This brings you to a large field – head towards a clump of trees 250 yards down the right side. Tucked away to the right of these trees is a stile leading into another field. Walk down the left side of this into Kirk Ireton.

2. On the road in the village turn left. Then bear right and walk down Main Street past the Barley Mow. At the bottom is the church. Where the road bears right here follow the Wirksworth road round to the left behind the church. Just beyond the churchyard is a driveway on the left then a squeezer stile. Pass through this and

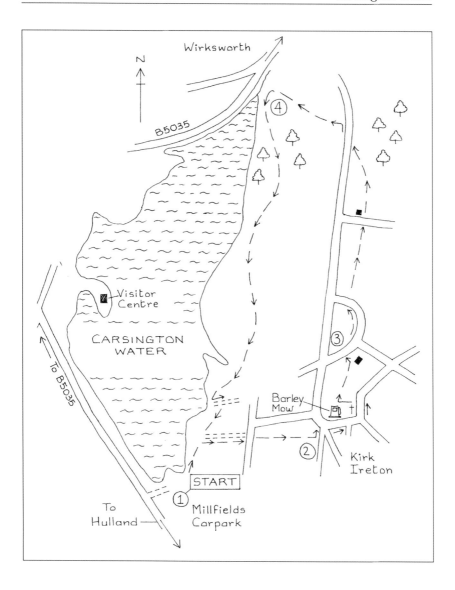

walk away from the lane. Keep in the same direction through a second and third field. After passing through a stile into the fourth field turn right under the electricity lines. Halfway along the hedge on the right pass through a stile onto the opposite side of the fence – continuing in the same direction. Cross a small watercourse and continue to a stile in the left corner. Cross this and walk to the far

63

right corner. Turn right along the driveway beyond. Immediately before the drive enters the property turn left through the stile. Walk up the right side of this fairly steep field to the top corner.

3. Turn right along the lane. Some 180 yards later keep forward into Halfmoon Lane, leaving Topshill Lane as it bears right. About 400 yards after joining this lane it begins to descend gently. Look out on the right at this point for a squeezer stile tucked behind a holly tree. Pass through this and walk along the right side of four fields. In the fifth bear slightly left to a stile. In the large (sixth) field walk parallel to the field boundary on the left to the farmgate 300 yards ahead – this is to the right of the cottage on the hillside in front. Cross the lane and pass through a stile ahead. Walk on the right side of two fields to reach Stainsborough Lane. Turn right here for 250 yards past Rough Pitty Side (a wood) on the right. At the stile on the left pass through. Walk forward into the field, keeping left of a hollow with three or four beeches in it. Proceed towards the wall ahead but start to bear right so that you descend the field with the wall that was in front of you now on your left. Ahead the village of Hopton should come into view. In the bottom left corner of the field pass through a stile. Walk straight forward in the next field and pass through a broken line of trees (and over a ditch). From here bear slightly left to the stile across the field. This brings you to the northern tip of Carsington Water.

4. Turn left on the gravel track and follow this as it rises into delightful Hall Wood. Keep on the track out of the wood to reach another tarmac lane over a mile later. Turn left up this before turning right off it opposite the buildings of Upperfield Farm. Follow the yellow waymarks which indicate the 'walking' route (as opposed to the cycling route). This should bring you to a bat shelter with examples of local timber. Just beyond this join the cycle route which soon brings you back to Hays Lane. Turn left up this then almost immediately right on the gravel path back to the start.

PLACES OF INTEREST NEARBY
Carsington Water Visitor Centre with its exhibition, shops and Barrowdale Restaurant is worth visiting. There's the chance to hire cycles or go trout fishing. If you take your binoculars do visit the bird hides – over 120 different species of bird have been seen.

WALK 14

HOLLOWAY AND
THE CROMFORD CANAL

*The walk includes a gentle 2 miles or so along the Cromford Canal.
The route then becomes a bit of an up-and-downer but this is a
smashing area with good views of the Derwent Valley.*

Highpeak Junction on the Cromford Canal

Holloway is perhaps best known for its connection, at Lea Hurst,
with Florence Nightingale. She lived there for some years and was,
of course, remembered for tending to wounded soldiers during the
Crimean War.

Part of the route runs alongside the Cromford Canal and this
provides an easy, flat mid-section to your walk. Cromford Wharf
marks one end of the canal – the other originally being near
Eastwood (D.H. Lawrence's birthplace) some fourteen miles away.
Most of the canal is still visible albeit silted up in places.

The Yew Tree Inn in Holloway (telephone: 01629 534355) is a good source of refreshment. The food is traditional, and there are daily specials too. The beers including Wards, Waggle Dance and Samson, are well kept. Strongbow and Woodpecker ciders are available if you prefer. Food is served from 12 noon to 2 pm (longer in summer) and 7 pm to 9 pm (in summer 6 pm to 9 pm). The pub is open for drinks for similar times during the day but longer in the evenings, closing at 10.30 pm on Sunday, 11 pm on other days.

- **HOW TO GET THERE:** Holloway is 3 miles south-east of Matlock. From the crossroads on the A6 at Cromford follow the signs for Holloway. The Yew Tree is at the top of Mill Lane on the right.
- **PARKING:** Park either in the car park of the Yew Tree (please let the landlord know) or on the opposite side of the road.
- **LENGTH OF THE WALK:** 6¼ miles. Map: OS Outdoor Leisure 24 White Peak area (GR 324563).

THE WALK

Please note that after heavy rain the stepping stones over Littlemoor Brook can flood (point 3 of the walk). Be prepared to either paddle or wear wellies!

1. Walk uphill from the pub. Turn right into Bracken Lane and descend for 300 yards. Immediately beyond Bracken Cottage turn sharp right on the footpath beside the garden. Turn left through the large metal gate. Descend gently down the track beside the wall to a cottage on the left. Beyond this descend beside the fence to another high gate. Pass through and turn left to the canal. Then turn left through the tunnel. Continue beside the canal for ¾ mile. Just before the tall pumping station chimney cross the footbridge and proceed with the canal on your left. Keep beside the canal for the next 1½ miles, passing High Peak Junction as you go – this marks the junction of the High Peak Trail and the Canal. When you reach Cromford Wharf, walk through the car park to the road.

2. Turn right and pass the church on the left. Cross the roadbridge. Follow the road round to the right – signposted Lea, Holloway and Crich. Pass the railway station. Walk under the railway bridge and 30 yards later turn left over the stile. Walk up the right side of the field. Ignore the path into the wood on the right after 200 yards. Continue

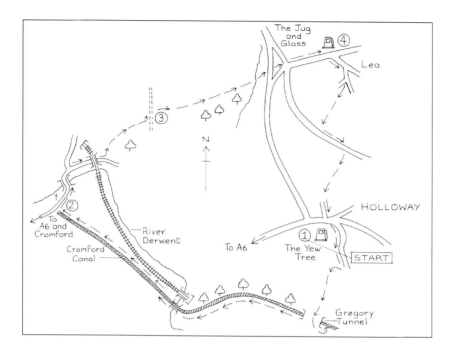

uphill with the wood on the right. Pass a spoil heap. Cross a track
and climb a stile. Bear half right up the field ahead. Keep forward
alongside the wall on the right. Towards the top of the field follow
the line of electricity posts to walk up the left side of the next field.
Pass through a squeezer stile into the wood. Follow the path beside
the wall. When the path leaves the wallside ignore a minor path to
the left. Continue under the beech trees onto a track.

3. Turn left for 60 yards. Then turn right over a stile. Walk down the
right side of the field. Cross a stile and continue down the right side
of the field beyond. Turn right at the wall corner. Pass through the
gap in the hedge 50 yards away. Then descend half left to the
bottom right corner of the next field. Walk down the right side of
the next field but bear slightly left in the one after to cross a stile by
a gate. Beyond this keep in the same direction, descending more
steeply. Pass through the hedge and head towards the bottom left
hand side of the field below. Follow a track climbing slightly uphill.
Just before the track bears left towards a farm turn right through a
stile. Bear left to follow the path through trees to another squeezer

The canalside path

stile. Pass through this and bear right to descend to Littlemoor Brook. Cross this by the stepping stones. Walk up the right side of the field ahead. Cross the road to the stile opposite. Rise up through the small field to the right of the little stone building at the top. Ignore the lane descending to the left – walk up the main road ahead towards the Jug and Glass.

4. Once there fork right into Holt Lane and walk uphill. Take the first turn right. Continue forward, rising gently along the road to reach Holt House. Take the track to the left of this and 100 yards later turn right down the surfaced path, signed 'Holloway' – at present! Keep beside the high stone wall for some distance to a lane. Turn left here. Continue for 500 yards, passing a war memorial tucked away on the right as you go. Take the surfaced bridleway on the right. Descend to the chapel, dated 1852. Turn left on the lane. Walk forward. At the T-junction turn right, back to the Yew Tree.

PLACES OF INTEREST NEARBY

Crich Tramway Museum is just over a mile away (telephone: 01773 852565) or if you head down into Cromford you can visit Arkwright's *Cromford Mill* (telephone: 01629 824297).

MAPLETON: BESIDE BENTLEY BROOK, THE RIVER DOVE AND HENMORE BROOK

A quiet corner of Derbyshire where you can get away from it all. Towards the end there's a marvellous view of the Dove Valley and Staffordshire. Before that you walk beside two brooks and the lower reaches of the River Dove.

The River Dove near Hanging Bridge

Mapleton, pronounced 'Mappleton', is a one street village running parallel to the River Dove just a field away. The town of Ashbourne nearby is worth exploring with its fine buildings such as the church and the old grammar school. Try to avoid it on Shrove Tuesday and Ash Wednesday when the annual Shrovetide football match is played – unless you want to watch. Be warned that the game isn't

restricted to a football pitch – it takes place anywhere in town as the
Uppards and Downards try and score against each other. As far as I
know, the rules (if there are any) are fairly loosely applied.

The Okeover Arms in Mapleton is open from 11.30 am to 3 pm
and 6 pm to 11 pm during the week and all day at the weekend – at
least in the summer, on cold winter days though they may be rather
more flexible. Telephone first if you want to check (01335 350305).
It's a nice pub with Ind Coope Burton Ale, Ansells Best Bitter and
Tetley on sale as well as Dry Blackthorn cider. There's good food
like rump steak, grilled Dove trout, grilled gammon and cheese and
tomato quiche to choose from too.

- **HOW TO GET THERE:** Mapleton is 1½ miles north-west of
  Ashbourne between the A52 Leek road and the A515 Buxton road.
- **PARKING:** There's only one village street so you can't miss the
  Okeover Arms. Park in the street nearby or ask permission to use
  the pub car park while you walk, if you are a customer.
- **LENGTH OF THE WALK:** 6¼ miles. Map: OS Pathfinder 810
  Ashbourne and the Churnet Valley (GR 165480).

THE WALK
1. With your back to the Okeover Arms turn left along the road.
Follow this for ¾ mile. Ignore paths to left and right. At a left hand
bend just after the road has started to rise fork right on a track
beside a wood. At the end of the track cross a stile. With your back
to the stile walk to the hedge corner ahead. Then bear slightly left to
a gate beside the Dove. Walk alongside the river through this field.
At the far end cross the stile and walk down the left side of the field
to cross a footbridge over Bentley Brook. Walk right alongside this.
Towards the end of the field cross a stile tucked away behind some
trees on the right. Then bear left to cross a stile. Climb up onto the
flood banking. Turn right along this, cross a stile and continue for
200 yards to the Dove – with Staffordshire beyond.

2. Turn left, passing through the squeezer stile into the field – do
not take the stile beside the river. Stay on the right side of three
fields to a farmgate. Cross the stile and proceed down the right side
of a car park. Walk past the Royal Oak Hotel on the left. Turn right
over Hanging Bridge into Staffordshire. Turn left on the Uttoxeter
road on the far side and 100 yards later bear left on a track leading

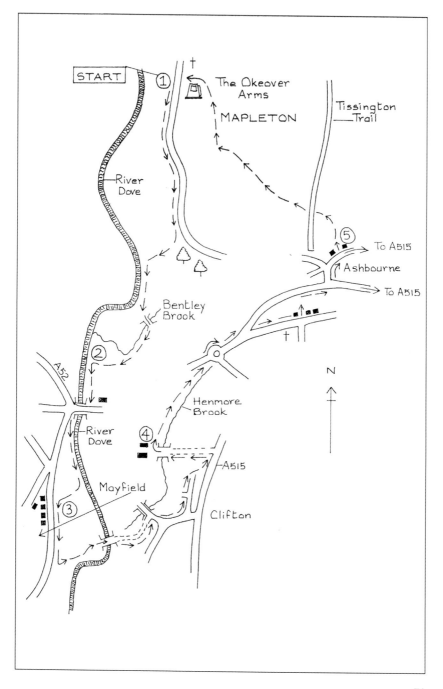

to the river. Follow the clear path past Hanging Bridge Sewage Pumping Station. Continue beside the river for 400 yards to some steps beside the water's edge leading up to a stile. Enter the playing fields beyond. Walk towards the red slate roofs of the houses ahead. Leave the playing fields by the entrance to the right of these houses.

3. Turn left along the road, passing the terraced houses of Weirside and then Meadowside. The road bears right. Just past the bend, opposite Dove Cottage, turn left down a path between fences. Follow this down to cross a millstream. Immediately beyond the footbridge turn left for 10 yards then right into The Terrace. Follow the road between the houses. At the end of South View pass Tattons Mill Sewage Pumping Station. The Dove is now on the right. Cross the bridge back into Derbyshire. Follow the access road as it bends left to a road. Turn right at the T-junction. Opposite are the old and new Downards goals for the Shrovetide football game. Ascend to another T-junction. Turn left here past the Cock Inn. Stay on the pavement on the left side of the road, passing the church hall. Ignore the road as it bears right up to the main road. Stay on the pavement, passing Clifton C of E School then the entrance to Cross Side. Rise slowly, ignoring a left fork, to come out beside the main road. Proceed, but immediately past Cross Cottage turn left down Green Lane. Stay on this for $1/4$ mile to reach Henmore Brook in front of Doles Farm. Cross the bridge on the right.

4. Immediately beyond turn right on the far side of the brook between the brook and the brick building. Walk beside the brook past the farm buildings on the left. Walk along the banking on the right side of the field beyond. Bear right 300 yards into the field to a stile beside a roundabout. Follow the road into Ashbourne past the cemetery on the left. Pass St Oswald's church – well worth a visit. At the end of the churchyard with School Lane on the right walk up the steps on the left side of the road. At the top turn right along the road to a T-junction. Turn left and follow the road as it bears right into North Avenue.

5. Opposite The Channel turn left on the Thorpe footpath. In the field bear half right to a stile. Continue in the same direction in the second field to the bottom right corner. In the third field aim three-quarters of the way down the right hand hedge. Beyond the hedge turn left downhill to the bridge. Cross this and turn left for 3 yards then fork right up the slope to the Tissington Trail. Cross this to a path on the far side. Descend into the field and walk up to the top right corner. Walk up the left side of the next field, bearing slightly right at the top to a farmgate. Keep down the right side of the next field, bearing right off the gravel track after 30 yards to cross a stile. Walk down the right side of the next field. In the field after this with Okeover Hall in the distance head slightly to the right of it. Pass through a stile and walk down the right side of the field to a gap – sometimes muddy. Turn right through this and walk on the top side of the field with a hedge on the right. Keep in the same direction through the next two fields towards the church. Pass through a stile in the far corner of the field behind the church. Walk through the churchyard back to the road and the start.

PLACES OF INTEREST NEARBY

The interesting and unusual church in the village itself is worth exploring as is the *church of St Oswald in Ashbourne*. If you want to travel 10 miles south of Ashbourne then *Sudbury Hall* is a marvellous National Trust property. The National Trust Museum of Childhood is housed in the Hall and this contains exhibitions about children from the 18th century onwards including a school classroom as it used to be. Telephone: 01283 585305.

GOLDEN VALLEY, THE CROMFORD CANAL AND IRONVILLE RESERVOIR

A walk full of hidden delights such as Ironville Reservoir, the old cobbled path rising up through the wood into Riddings, the centre of Riddings itself and the Cromford Canal. All in an area with a fascinating industrial history.

The Cromford Canal

The route takes you alongside a lovely section of the Cromford Canal which flows into Ironville Reservoir. You then follow the line of the Pinxton Canal although you may not realise it as it is completely filled in. Still there are some clues to its existence in the roadbridges you pass under. You also pass through the outskirts of Ironville, a 19th-century model village built by the Butterley Company. Riddings, which comes a little later, is a surprise. Most visitors will probably only know the newer, rather anonymous, buildings on the main road. However half a mile or so away is the old part of the village – complete with thatched pub (and there can't be many of them in Derbyshire) – The Moulders' Arms – and just across the road is the Seven Stars pub.

The Newlands Inn, where the walk starts, offers home-cooked food from a cheese burger to 'Drunken Bull with Mash'. Or why not try the lamb, leek and mushroom casserole? Theakston XB, Home Bitter plus guests are available as well. For opening times, telephone: 01773 744244.

- **HOW TO GET THERE:** Golden Valley is 1½ miles north-east of Ripley. From Codnor on the A610 between Ripley and Eastwood take the road north for Ironville and Riddings. The Newlands Inn is clearly visible on the left shortly after entering Golden Valley.
- **PARKING:** There is a large car park at the Newlands Inn. For those walkers not wishing to use the pub after the walk, turn right just before the Newlands Inn for Ironville. There is a small car park on the left after about 750 yards. (Note: this is the car park referred to in the fourth line of the walk directions.)
- **LENGTH OF THE WALK:** 5½ miles. Map: OS Pathfinder 795 Sutton in Ashfield (GR 423512).

The Walk

1. Cross the road from the inn. Turn right, ignore the road signed 'Golden Valley', then turn to follow the path for Pinxton beside the canal. Pass under a bridge. Later cross a footbridge on the right into a car park. Cross this and join the path running on the right bank of Ironville Reservoir. About 500 yards later enter another car park. Cross the footbridge and continue to the end of the reservoir and turn left. Here there's a good view up the length of the reservoir. Some 150 yards later ignore the steps ahead – turn right along disused Pinxton Canal – there's hardly anything of it left. With houses to the right pass under a low footbridge. Stay on the obvious path to reach an open area. Keep forward past the cemetery on the left and the church on the right. Pass under a low roadbridge. Stay on the path with houses on the right and pass under the railway bridge. Continue forward, ignoring paths to left and right. Follow the path through a narrow band of woodland. This is still along the disused canal.

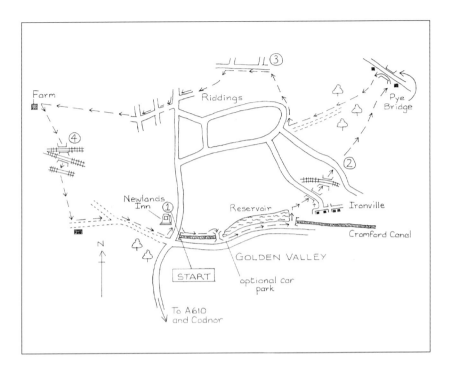

2. Cross a road and 350 yards later ignore a crosspath. Then pass a pond on the left. Subsequently walk alongside a pebble-dashed house on the right. At the end of the house proceed to the road – this is Pye Bridge. Turn left over the roadbridge then immediately left on the far side along a drive. Keep forward after a few yards as the drive bears right. Follow the tall fencing on the right past the pond you saw earlier. The path bears right and uphill. Cross the entrance to the timber merchants and continue beyond. The path rises through woodland on marvellous old cobbles to pass under two bridges. At the tarmac lane continue forward uphill. About 150 yards later pass houses on the left and continue forward. Ignore a lane to the left. Pass the chapel, dated 1838, on the right. Turn right at the T-junction and keep right into Church Street past the Moulders' Arms, then the Seven Stars with a fascinating explanation of the origin of its name. Proceed past an old terrace of brick houses. At No 31 turn right on the footpath along Park Mews. After a few yards at the private entrance to Park Mews there is a sight of the hexagonal Granary. Keep on the path into Riddings

Park – a country park rather than a town park. Walk forward to reach a road (Parkside) running uphill to the left.

3. Walk up this for 300 yards. Just past Ward Drive on the right turn left on the tarmac path until it forks. Take the right fork into an open grassy area. This path leads to a parking area. Continue across it into and along Shaw Street to the main street of Riddings 100 yards ahead. Turn left for 50 yards. Cross the road and follow the path for Swanwick and Butterley along the lane opposite the hardware store. Stay on this between properties, continuing along Peak Avenue beyond. Ignore Dale Avenue and Lea Crescent. Bear left just past Peveril Drive and cross the footbridge over the disused railway cutting. Walk on the right side of six fields beyond to reach Hillside Farm. Look out to the left for a brick chimney (an airshaft) which you'll pass later. At the end of the last field keep on the right side of the lawn to the driveway. As soon as you reach the drive turn left along it to reach the corner of a stone wall – just 15 yards from where you entered this lawned area. Follow the path for Golden Valley for 1/2 mile along the track, heading towards the airshaft ahead. To the right is the Midland Railway Centre.

4. Pass under a railway bridge and under another on the right 75 yards later. Go up the path beyond. Ignore a stile on the left after 15 yards to cross a railway line – 'stop, look and listen' here! Ascend the narrow path beyond (ignoring the wider track to its right). This path leads past the airshaft on the right. At the end of the fencing turn right then immediately left down the path through the trees. At the bottom cross a narrow bridge and walk up the left side of a field. Cross a tarmac drive to a stile. Follow the path on the left side of the next field to cross a stile to Butterley Park Farm. Turn left down the tarmac lane, passing the farm on your right. Continue down here, ignoring the sharp turn left to the Midland Railway Centre. At Newlands Road turn left, back to the inn.

PLACES OF INTEREST NEARBY

The obvious place to visit is, of course, the *Midland Railway Centre*. Alternatively drive 4 miles south to visit the *Denby Potteries* or 5 or 6 miles south-east to *D. H. Lawrence's birthplace* at Eastwood.

WALK 17

DUFFIELD AND ALLESTREE PARK: BESIDE THE RIVER DERWENT

An interesting walk on the northern side of Derby with a few surprises such as Allestree Hall with its tranquil lake and an enjoyable stretch of path beside the River Derwent towards the end.

Allestree Park

The walk starts in the village of Duffield which stands on the A6, busy with traffic the road carries between Derby and the Peak District. It has some interesting buildings, including Duffield Hall which is the headquarters of the Derbyshire Building Society. Standing on the hillside above Duffield is Quarndon – a quieter village with a chalybeate well, the basis in the 17th and 18th centuries for Quarndon's ambition to be a spa town to rival Buxton. The walk then passes through Allestree Park in the middle of which is Allestree Hall. The route subsequently runs alongside a small lake

78

in the parkland which is usually full of wildfowl – look out for kingfishers.

The White Hart in Duffield offers a traditional no-nonsense pub atmosphere with good beer (Pedigree, Bass and occasional guests such as Old Speckled Hen and Ruddles County) plus good food (soup, sandwiches, home-made steak and kidney pie, fisherman's pie, plaice and scampi). It's open from 11.30 am to 3 pm and 6 pm to 11 pm on Monday to Saturday and from 12 noon to 3 pm and 7 pm to 10.30 pm on Sunday. Food is served from 12 noon until 2 pm every day and from 6 pm to 9 pm on Wednesday, Thursday, Friday and Saturday. Telephone: 01332 841141.

- **HOW TO GET THERE:** Duffield is 5 miles north of Derby on the A6. The White Hart is beside the main road in the middle of the village.
- **PARKING:** You can park in the pub car park or in one of the streets nearby.
- **LENGTH OF THE WALK:** 6½ miles. Map: OS Pathfinder 811 'Belper' (GR 345433).

THE WALK

1. Face the front of the White Hart. Turn left along the road, then right on Wirksworth Road. Just before the entrance to Ecclesbourne School turn left on the path between houses, nos. 45 and 47. Continue along the road beyond. At the staggered crossroads turn right. Turn left at the T-junction to the main road at the top.

2. Cross this to the access road running parallel to the main road. Turn left, then right immediately beyond Stoneleigh on the Quarndon path. Walk forward in the field and proceed on the left side of the hedge in front. Duffield is soon left behind. In the second field turn right. In the third continue to a stile by the gate opposite. Follow the grassy track beyond to a gateway. Continue beside a hedge on the right to a stile in the top right corner. Veer slightly left towards a hedge/fence corner jutting out ahead. Continue alongside the hedge to cross a stile. In the next field walk to the top right corner. Pass through the stile to cross a track. Walk up the left side of the trees ahead and a wood to a driveway. Bear right to the road at Quarndon Common.

3. Turn left and ½ mile later near the church look out for the village

79

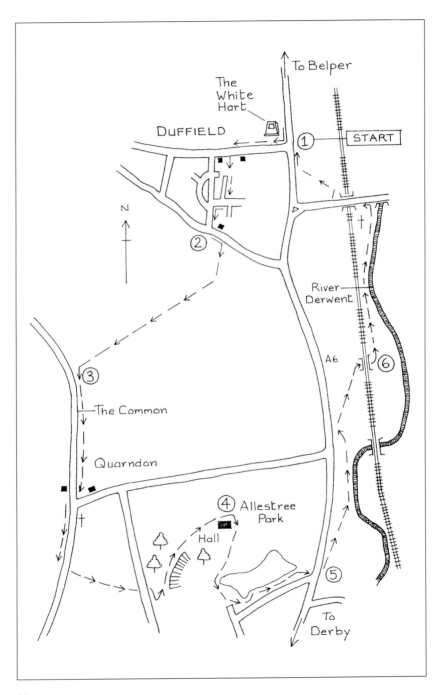

Canada geese by the lake in Allestree Park

map. Bear right downhill, signposted for Kedleston and Derby. Pass Barn Close. Turn left immediately before the high wall at house no. 74. Walk down the right side of the field past the cottage. Climb the stile at the end of the field. There's a delightful garden over the wall. Ascend the right side of the field. To the left is a water tower prominent for miles around. Pass through the gap in the hedge on the right. Continue in the same direction as before with the hedge on your left. At the end of the hedge bear slightly left up the field ahead. Follow a track to the lane. Turn right to the small car park. Turn left into this. Keep on the left side of it and walk directly away from the road. Follow the wide path, ignoring a smaller one forking left after a few yards. The path bears left into the trees. It subsequently bears round to the right with a very large hollow to the right – keep this on your right! Walk under yew trees to the seat on the edge of the wood. Give way to golfers before crossing to a small wood 30 yards away. Walk down the left side of this – descending as you go. Try and keep beside the trees. After 200 yards turn right along the track towards the high fenced animal pens, usually full of birds and animals. Keep these to your left and walk towards Allestree Hall – the home of Allestree Golf Club.

4. Pass the Hall on the access road and 80 yards later where the access road bears left turn right on the tarmac path. Stay on this for some distance to a road stretching away ahead. Turn left before this on the gravel path to the lake. Walk down the right side to the far end. Bear right to the road 50 yards away. Turn left to the A6.

5. Cross this carefully and turn left for 30 yards. Immediately past the last driveway fork right. Descend below the level of the road. Enter a field. Proceed through the hawthorns, then a pair of redundant gateposts. Keep forward to the farmgate and pass through the stile. Walk to a stile by a farmgate to the right of the bungalow. Cross this and turn half right. Pass through a stile between two gates and turn left beside the fence with outbuildings on the other side. Pass a steeply roofed brick building on the left. Continue alongside a fence and 100 yards past this building cross a footbridge on the left. Turn right beyond to walk beside the river. Cross a stile and then another on a bend in the river. Keep forward with a ditch on the right. Eventually cross a footbridge on the right. Beyond, aim for the tall chimney $1/2$ mile away. Pass a tree in the middle of the field with a piece of ornate stonework at the bottom. Keep in the same direction to a stile. Bear slightly left beyond. Pass through the fence, continuing in the same direction to a stile leading under the railway line.

6. On the other side turn left parallel to the line. Cross a stile by two rounded gateposts. Bear slightly right to a gap in an embankment. Then bear just right of the church ahead to cross a stile. Turn right to the river. Continue along the river bank. Pass through the churchyard. Keep on the right side of the field beyond. Follow the path to the road. Turn left, crossing the railway line. Immediately beyond turn right and descend into the field. Follow the obvious path across the field to the A6. Turn right, back to the start.

PLACES OF INTEREST NEARBY
Besides *Derby* itself you could visit 18th-century *Kedleston Hall*, 3 miles south-west of Duffield, (telephone: 01332 842191), or *Belper*, 4 miles to the north.

WALK 18

ELVASTON CASTLE AND THE
RIVER DERWENT

The shortest walk in the book – and there are no hills. Right on the edge of Derby this is a fascinating stroll in a surprisingly rural setting. You can't fail to be impressed not just by Elvaston Castle and the Golden Gates but the unlikelier Borrowash Weir and the sluice gates too!

The River Derwent

Elvaston Castle Country Park was apparently one of the first of its kind and provides an interesting and flat walk near to Derby. The Golden Gates which you pass towards the end of the circuit are predominantly blue and were alleged to have been taken by Napoleon from a palace in Madrid and subsequently acquired by the Earl of Harrington, possibly as 'spoils of war'. Suffice to say they are impressive. The castle is partly 17th-century with additions made

83

during the 19th century. The gardens are worth exploring after the walk – with Derbyshire County Council doing their best to keep them in good condition.

For refreshment I suggest visiting Mrs Kemps, a tea room situated in Elvaston Castle. This is open 364 days a year from 9.30 am to 5 or 6 pm (later at weekends) in summer. In winter it's usually open from 10 am until 3.30 pm. The range of food runs from the smallest snack to a full blown meal, and you can choose from dishes such as baked potato, omelette, sandwiches or hot pot, mushroom stroganoff and tuna pasta bake. For those walkers who've got to have a glass of beer there is a choice of bottles! Telephone: 01332 755796.

- **HOW TO GET THERE:** Elvaston Castle Country Park is $4^1/_2$ miles south-east of Derby. From the A6 south of Derby turn northwards on the B5010 towards Borrowash to reach the car park for the country park on the left further along this road.
- **PARKING:** Park in the Elvaston Castle Country Park Visitors' Car and Caravan Park.
- **LENGTH OF THE WALK:** $4^1/_2$ miles. Map: OS Pathfinders 832 Derby and Etwall and 833 Nottingham (South West) (GR 413332).

THE WALK

1. From the car park walk back towards the road and 30 yards before it turn left along the gravel path beneath the trees. Continue parallel to the road to reach a driveway. Turn right to the road then left along it for $1/_3$ mile. At the tarmac lane on the left turn left to follow the gravel track on the left side of the lane. Stay on this as it bears right towards the River Derwent. Bear left and walk beside the river. Take the right fork beside the weir. This path is surprisingly rural.

2. At the flood barrier (Spondon Sluices) fork left away from the river along the cinder track towards the houses in the distance. Follow this track through the houses to reach some school grounds on the left. Stay on the track between the school on the left and houses on the right. This brings you to the entrance of St John Fisher RC Primary School. Turn left on the road beyond the school. Ignore all roads to right and then left to reach St Michael and All Angels church.

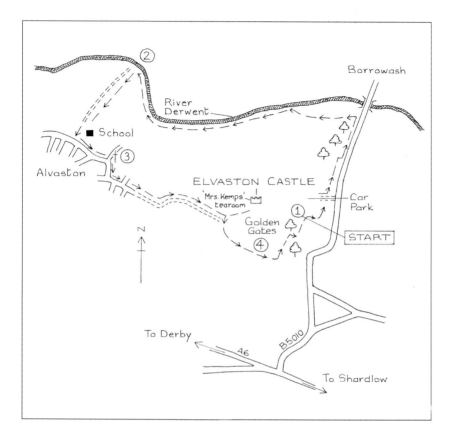

3. Bear right into Church Street. Pass Church Farm on the right. At the T-junction turn left. At the roundabout 150 yards later keep forward (signed 'Bridleway to Elvaston'). Ignore the left turn into Stocker Avenue. Pass Sledmore Close on the right and keep forward into Elvaston Lane. Stay on this bridleway through the houses to reach the countryside again. Just beyond Castle Lodge and The Lodge re-enter Elvaston Castle Country Park. Keep forward, ignoring paths to left and right. About 300 yards later with a small redbrick bridge over a ditch ahead turn right along the bridleway. Turn left after 200 yards. Where the bridleway joins a tarmac drive keep forward with Elvaston County Cricket Ground to the left. The bridleway then passes an attractive mature garden on the left with a more natural wood on the right.

85

The Golden Gates

4. The magnificent Golden Gates appear next on the left – even though they're mainly blue! Pass these and continue along the tarmac drive. Some 120 yards later at the end of the lawn on the left u rn left on the wide gravel path into the trees. Follow this round to the right as it narrows, ignoring a narrower path straight ahead. Then turn left and follow the path just inside the edge of the country park. The path bears right then left to bring you to the walled English Garden. Walk along the left side of this bearing right to a small holly tree in the middle of the path. Bear right beyond this along a tarmac drive, passing various brick outbuildings on the right. With the road about 50 yards ahead of you turn left through the gateway along the gravel track. Walk back to the car park parallel to the road. As you proceed you'll see a delightful view of the castle down to the left through the trees.

PLACES OF INTEREST NEARBY
In addition to *Elvaston Castle* with its fascinating Estate Museum (telephone: 01332 571342), there's the city of *Derby* with plenty to do!

TRENT LOCK, THE RIVER TRENT
AND THE EREWASH CANAL

There is marvellous walking hereabouts. This is a flat walk, alongside the Cranfleet Canal, then the River Trent and later by the Erewash Canal – with all the happy comings and goings of assorted river and canal craft to entertain you as you stroll along.

Trent Lock where the Erewash Canal joins the River Trent

Trent Lock is a quiet spot, just a couple of pubs, a tea room and assorted houseboats. Even so it's always a popular and interesting place for visitors both by road and water. There are usually some narrowboats moving slowly by. Later, the walk enters Long Eaton. The Erewash Canal that passes through the town is a delight for those who want to explore somewhere a little different. The old redbrick lace mills by the canal are still in use in most cases and provide an attractive architectural backdrop to the canal itself.

The Trent Navigation Inn, in a lovely spot beside the Trent and near the canal, is a pub full of atmosphere. It's also a dog-friendly pub with a room where you can take your best friend – the furry one. It also gets very busy at weekends. It opens from 11.30 am to 11 pm every day except Sunday when the hours are from 12 noon until 10.30 pm. Food is available at lunchtime from 11.30 am to 2 pm on Monday to Saturday and 12 noon to 3 pm on Sunday and from 6.30 pm to 9 pm every evening. Theakstons Best Bitter is on sale plus Pedigree and Home Mild with Strongbow and Woodpecker ciders. There's a guest beer (such as Ruddles County) which is changed about every fortnight. The food includes Cumberland Ring, scampi, 24oz rump steaks, broccoli bake and spring rolls plus mixed grills for the person with a healthy appetite. Telephone: 0115 9732984.

- **HOW TO GET THERE:** Trent Lock is 1½ miles due south of Long Eaton and may not be marked on some road maps. Follow the B6540 from Long Eaton south-west towards Shardlow and 1¾ miles from Long Eaton town centre turn left along Lock Lane for Trent Lock. Continue to the car park at the end of the lane on the right.
- **PARKING:** There is a large free car park at Trent Lock.
- **LENGTH OF THE WALK:** 6¼ miles. Map: OS Pathfinder 833 Nottingham (South West) (GR 489313).

THE WALK

1. From the car park at the end of Lock Lane turn right past the back of the Trent Navigation Inn. Bear left in front of it and then right at the building dated 1950. Keep to the right of the lock at the end of the Erewash Canal leading into the River Trent. Cross the footbridge and follow the gravel path beyond alongside the river for a short distance. Then bear left along the Cranfleet Canal. Away to the right is Redhill Railway Tunnel with Ratcliffe-on-Soar Power Station beyond. Stay by the canal for ¾ mile to reach Cranfleet Lock. Beyond this proceed along the gravel path beside the river. After passing through a gateway bear right, ignoring a path forking left. The path to the right is a long, straight one over 200 yards in length. Initially the high ground of Gotham Hill can be seen straight ahead. As the river meanders this hillside will subsequently be on your right and then behind you. Pass a largish fishing lake on your left. The river bends left and then right. As you pass a second

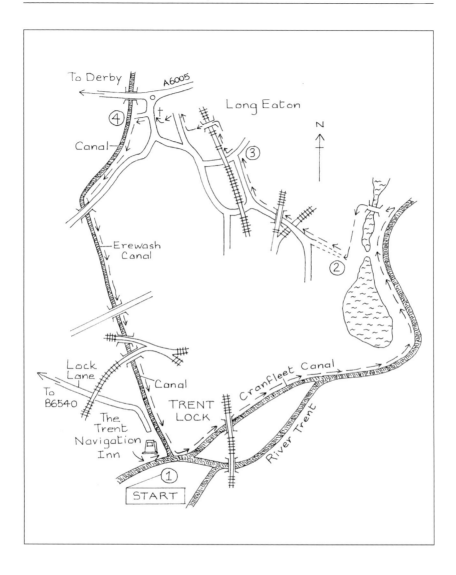

(smaller) pond on the left (though it is sometimes connected to the first one depending on the depth of water) look out for a footbridge ahead to the left. This has to be crossed but only after the path you're on appears to have passed it. So, after crossing a stile turn sharp left to the footbridge 100 yards away. This is part of the Trent Valley Way. The path beyond the bridge leads into Trent Meadows. Where it emerges into the open from amongst the trees and shrubs

89

A narrowboat joining the Erewash Canal

ignore the first path to the left alongside the pond. Walk forward for 20 yards towards the electricity lines. Then turn left along the grassy track running along the bottom of a grassy embankment. This track runs parallel to the pond 30 yards to your left. After 350 yards turn right into the car park.

2. Walk straight through this to its entrance. Continue along the road ahead to enter the outskirts of Long Eaton. Cross the railway line. Ignore roads to left and right. Pass under a railway bridge. As the road bears right stay on it but at a mini-roundabout keep forward along New Tythe Street. Walk along this for 400 yards.

3. At the T-junction turn left but immediately before crossing the railway line turn right along a path to wind past the back of houses on the right. Cross the railway line by a footbridge. At the bottom follow the path to the road ahead. Turn right here. Keep forward at the roundabout, passing Waverley Mills across the road on the right. Ignore the road to the left but 120 yards beyond the roundabout take the footpath leading down the left side of the church. The church may be locked but the churchyard is a relatively quiet place to stop for a while. Continue onto the main street beyond the church, coming out opposite the Old Bell pub. Turn right then left into Regent Street. Walk along this for 300 yards to the Erewash Canal.

4. Turn left along the canal and follow it for the next 2 miles back to Trent Lock but watch out for bikes! It's worth enjoying some of the features of the canal. For instance after you first reach it there is the attractive brick mill on the opposite side. The canal runs alongside the road just before getting back to the outskirts of the town. The countryside is soon reached though and the cooling towers of the power station are visible. Towards the end of the walk there are a number of houseboats moored by the side of the canal. The walk ends in the vicinity of the Steamboat Inn from which point you should be able to find your way back to the start.

PLACES OF INTEREST NEARBY

The city of *Nottingham* lies 7 miles to the north-east. Or you could explore *Attenborough Nature Reserve*. This lies 3 miles north-east of Trent Lock on the southern side of the A6005 near the village of Attenborough. There's usually plenty of wildfowl about. The reserve is to the north of the ponds crossed by the route when walking from the River Trent. It is accessible by car.

WALK 20

TICKNALL AND
FOREMARK RESERVOIR

《❀》

The southernmost walk in this book in an increasingly popular area. Ticknall is an interesting village with its old lock-up and unique roadside water taps and Foremark Reservoir is well worth exploring.

Foremark Reservoir

The walk follows field paths to Foremark Reservoir where Burton Sailing Club operate and trout fishing is available (in season). The reservoir holds nearly 3000 million gallons of water and provides drinking water for the East Midlands. At the southern end of the reservoir is Carvers Rocks Nature Reserve through which the walk passes. On your return to Ticknall you will pass a number of green water taps (or pumps) by the roadside. These were provided by the Harpur Crewe family (from nearby Calke Abbey) for the villagers to draw their water. There's also an interesting lock-up towards the end

92

of the walk. The local pub landlady apparently had a key to this as well as the local 'bobby' and would often release anyone locked up for the night for being drunk and disorderly.

The Staff of Life in Ticknall is a lovely pub with good food and good beer. As regards the latter, Timothy Taylor Landlord, Shepherd Neame Spitfire, Pedigree, Bass and Boddingtons are all usually for sale. Then the food: there are specials like pork pieces in a rich ginger sauce or try the regular menu for scampi, fillets of plaice and mini breaded lobster tails, with broccoli and cheese bake or spinach and ricotta cannelloni for a vegetarian choice. The Staff of Life is open from 11.30 am to 2.15 pm and 6.30 pm to 10.15 pm on Monday to Saturday and from 12 noon to 2.15 pm and 7 pm to 10.30 pm on Sunday. Food is served throughout opening hours (to 10 pm on Sunday). A favourite pub for many, the Staff of Life can be very busy at weekends in particular. Telephone: 01332 862479.

- **HOW TO GET THERE:** Ticknall is on the A514 south of Derby.
- **PARKING:** From the main street turn up Ingleby Lane to the car park near the village hall.
- **LENGTH OF THE WALK:** 5½ miles. Map: OS Pathfinder 852 Burton upon Trent (GR 353241).

THE WALK

1. Cross the stile in the fence on the top side of the car park. Turn left and walk towards the church, crossing another stile to walk behind it. Ignore a stile on the left past the church. Keep forward over another stile and cross a track beyond. Continue beside the hedge on the left. Stay on the left side of a second and third field. At the end of this third field away to your right should be the buildings of Knowle Hill Farm. Walk on the left side of a fourth and fifth field, gradually descending in this last field to reach Hangman's Stone although there's nothing visible! Here a path crosses the bridleway you're on. Hanging and gibbeting often took place at crossroads and suicides were buried there. From here keep forward on the obvious bridleway now with a hedge on your right. Continue forward where you join a red sandy track coming in from the right. Head towards the power lines in front.

2. At the end of the field follow the bridleway round to the left, ignoring a less obvious bridleway running forward. Stay on the track

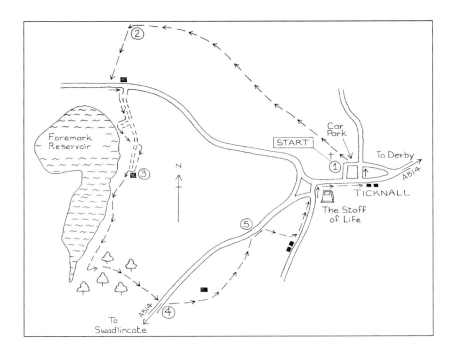

for 600 yards, passing a group of farm buildings on the right. Turn left when you reach the road to pass Bendalls Farm. Turn right beyond the farm along the entrance to Foremark Reservoir. Keep on the access road for 300 yards before bearing right – ignore the other access road leading forward. Rise up the slope to catch a first glimpse of the reservoir. Follow the road left into a car park. Walk to the far side of this and proceed on the path to an access road. Cross this into the play area and 20 yards later turn right through the woodland to another car park. Keep forward to the information centre beyond. There are toilets here!

3. Pass the centre and the picnic tables to enter another wood along a gravel path. After 50 yards walk forward across the open ground ahead. The reservoir is no more than 25 yards away. Keep to the left of the area reserved for anglers. Follow the gravel footpath for Carvers Rocks. This path descends and ascends before joining a path from the left – keep forward here. After descending some steps and subsequently some more, walk alongside some attractive fencing. The path rises via steps to continue along some duckboarding. Then

94

The old lock-up in Ticknall

cross a footbridge to reach an open area. Bear very slightly right to a gap in a fence to enter Carvers Rocks Nature Reserve. You are now nearly at the southern tip of the reservoir. Cross another footbridge to come very near the water. Cross another bridge over a small stream, fork left for 10 yards then bear slightly left uphill. Keep forward along the obvious path rising uphill through the wood. Ignore all other paths to left and right. Follow the path to an access road. Turn right and stay on it until it bends right. At this point keep straight forward on a short path leading to the road beyond.

4. Cross this, bearing slightly left to climb a stile. With your back to the road head half left across the field. This leads you to the right of the brick farmhouse ahead. To the right is Breedon-on-the-Hill church with Ratcliffe-on-Soar Power Station to the left of this. The path leads towards a large tree to the right of the field below the farm. Walk along the bottom side of this field with the farm uphill to the left. Cross a stile and walk quarter left towards the far left hand corner of the field past the farm orchard on the left. Cross the stile in the corner and walk on the left side of the next two fields. At the end of the second field cross a narrow footbridge. Bear half left to a gate beside a cottage leading onto the A514.

5. Turn right on the road for 100 yards. Climb a stile on the right and proceed across the field, keeping 10 yards to the left of the electricity pole ahead. In the next field bear very slightly left, heading towards the far right corner and Ticknall beyond. As you get nearer the corner follow the path to a stile beside a gate 20 yards to the right of the corner. This brings you to the road. Turn left, looking out for the green water pumps. Pass the Staff of Life and turn right at the T-junction just beyond. Keep on this road until you reach the Wheel pub where you should turn left up Ingleby Lane back to the car park.

PLACES OF INTEREST NEARBY
Calke Abbey (N.T.) stands in beautiful parkland on the southern edge of Ticknall. For real ale lovers why not drive a few miles west to *Burton upon Trent* and see if you can visit a brewery?